ROWE v. PACIFIC QUAD, INC.

Fourth Edition

ROWE V. PACIFIC QUAD, INC.

Fourth Edition

David Benjamin Oppenheimer

Professor of Law
Golden Gate University
School of Law
San Francisco, California

NATIONAL INSTITUTE FOR TRIAL ADVOCACY

Address inquiries to:

Reprint Permission
National Institute for Trial Advocacy
361 Centennial Parkway, Suite 220
Louisville, CO 80027
Phone: (800) 225-6482
www.nita.org

ISBN: 978-1-60156-049-0
FBA: 1049
11 10 09   10 9 8 7 6 5 4 3 2

Manufactured in the United States of America

Preface to the Fourth Edition

Though written before the Anita Hill hearings, the 1991 Civil Rights Act, and all but one of the Supreme Court's five major decisions on sexual harassment law, the Rowe case file has held up remarkably well. Nonetheless, by 2007 it was time for an update, if not an overhaul. Those who have used the first, second, or third editions will find most of the basic facts unchanged, but some fine-tuning of the material gives it a twenty-first century feel, plus a substantial re-writing of the legal memo (in the form of an appellate decision) brings the file into conformity with Title VII and California FEHA law. Because federal law and California law have deviated on the question of how the existence of an employer's anti-harassment policy affects liability, a choice of law election is provided in the new jury instructions. I'm indebted to my research assistant, Julie Ann Talbo, for her help in making these revisions.

May 2007
David Benjamin Oppenheimer
Professor of Law & Associate Dean for Faculty Development
Golden Gate University School of Law
San Francisco, California

Preface to the First Edition

This case file was originally written to be used in the Boalt Hall Employment Discrimination Clinic. The Clinic, founded in 1982, was sponsored by the California Department of Fair Employment and Housing and the University of California, Berkeley, School of Law (Boalt Hall). The Clinic combined the teaching of trial advocacy with the prosecution of actual civil rights cases before the California Fair Employment and Housing Commission. Clinic students, using the case file and problems drawn from their actual case load, performed weekly trial advocacy exercises as part of their course study at Boalt Hall. Then, under my supervision, they represented the Department of Fair Employment and Housing in contested evidentiary hearings before the Fair Employment and Housing Commission. The clinic closed in August 1986.

The case is set in Nita City, in the State of Nita, and is to be tried in the Superior Court of the County of Darrow. California substantive law is frequently used, and many of the citations to Nita statutes and cases in turn correspond to citations in the various California codes and cases in the California Reports and California Appellate Reports. The procedural aspects of the case, however, use federal law.

Major portions of this case file were written by my former research assistant, Ignatius Bau, Boalt Hall and Clinic graduate. Other contributors include Boalt Hall students Denise Abrams, Jeffrey B. Demain, Anne Kamsvaag, and Sam Miller. They deserve substantial credit for its success. Its limitations and liabilities, however, are entirely my responsibility. Special thanks are also due to our clinic secretary and literary consultant, Lois Schwartz.

July 1986
David Benjamin Oppenheimer
Berkeley, California

TABLE OF CONTENTS

EXHIBITS

INTRODUCTION

The plaintiff Alice Rowe has brought an action for sexual harassment and wrongful discharge against her employer, Pacific Quad, Inc. Ms. Rowe had worked for Pacific Quad for less than one week before walking off the job. She asserts that her supervisor, operations manager Stanley Schmit, continually leered at her, made offensive sexually suggestive comments to her, brushed by her in order to sexually touch her, and, finally, propositioned her. She further alleges that the president of Pacific Quad, John Walsh, was informed of the harassment and ratified it.

The defendant Pacific Quad denies that the harassment occurred. Pacific Quad is a small (twelve employee) software design company that creates software packages for medium-sized companies to help them improve the efficiency of their technology operations. Walsh and Schmit claim that Rowe was a highly nervous, marginally productive administrative assistant who was likely to be dismissed the week after she walked off the job. They claim to be mystified as to why she quit but speculate that she was paranoid or was extremely oversensitive and misunderstood the friendly atmosphere of their small, family-like office. Rowe had filed a sexual harassment claim, which was dismissed, against a professor when she was in college.

Rowe claims lost wages, medical expenses (psychotherapy), general damages for emotional distress, and punitive damages.

The applicable law is found in the Opinion of the Nita Court of Appeals and the Proposed Jury Instructions.

All years in these materials are stated in the following form:

YR -0 indicates the actual year in which the case is being tried (i.e., the present year);

YR -1 indicates the next preceding year (please use the actual year);

YR -2 indicates the second preceding year (please use the actual year), etc.

SPECIAL INSTRUCTIONS FOR USE AS A FULL TRIAL

Issues for Trial

This case file may be used for a full trial on the issue of liability only or on the issues of both liability and damages. If used solely for the issue of liability, the proposed jury instructions should be modified accordingly by deleting instructions 2.17–2.23, plus either 2.15 (to use federal law) or 2.16 (to use California law). Although the employer is too small to come under the federal anti-discrimination statute (Title VII), the case can be tried under a state law that adopts either the federal or California approach on what effect to give an employer's anti-harassment policies, by selecting the appropriate jury instruction. When using the file to try both liability and damages, to apply federal law, omit jury instructions 2.15 and 2.21; to apply California law, omit instruction 2.16.

Witnesses

When this case file is used for a full trial, the following witnesses are available to the parties:

For the plaintiff:	For the defendant:
Alice Rowe	John Walsh
Anna Mills	Stanley Schmit
Gloria Warner	Susan Robinson

A party need not call all of the witnesses listed as their witnesses. Any or all of the witnesses may be called by either party. However, if a witness is to be called by a party other than the one for whom he or she is listed, the party for whom the witness is listed will select the actor and prepare the witness.

Required Stipulations

1. The statements made in the edited depositions are admissible to the same extent as statements from full depositions.

2. The records of the Nita Department of Fair Employment and Housing, pages 63–85 of this case file, were supplied to the parties by the Nita Department of Fair Employment and Housing, pursuant to the Nita Public Records Act.

3. The Department of Fair Employment and Housing investigator, Annie Cunningham, is unavailable; she has taken a job on a Greenpeace ship and is somewhere in the Arctic Ocean.

Her notes were written in her role as a public employee and resulted from an investigation made pursuant to authority granted by law. These notes were made at the time of the conversation reported and were kept in the course of a regularly scheduled governmental activity. It was the regular practice of the Department of Fair Employment and Housing investigator to make such notes. The observations placed in the file were observed pursuant to her duty as imposed by the Nita Fair Employment and Housing Act, which requires state discrimination investigators to make a record of all conversations with complainants, respondents, and witnesses.

4. The diagram of the Pacific Quad offices is a true and accurate depiction of the office layout and is properly drawn to scale.

5. Statements or stipulations by counsel contained in the case file are binding on trial counsel.

6. On September 12, YR -2, Ms. Rowe began work as an administrative assistant for Business Systems, Inc., at a monthly salary of $3,500. Her lost wages for the period of her unemployment totaled twenty-four thousand five hundred dollars ($24,500).

IN THE SUPERIOR COURT OF DARROW COUNTY, NITA

CIVIL DIVISION

ALICE ROWE Plaintiff	)))	
	)	Civ. No. O-9876543
vs.	))	COMPLAINT
PACIFIC QUAD, INC., Defendant.	))	

Plaintiff ALICE ROWE, a resident and citizen of Nita City, State of Nita, herein alleges that Defendant PACIFIC QUAD, INC., a corporation duly incorporated and existing under and by virtue of the law of the State of Nita, with its domicile and principal place of business in the City of Nita, Darrow County, State of Nita, is liable to her for damages for the reasons that follow:

1. Stanley Schmit (hereinafter referred to as "Schmit") is, and at all times relevant to this action has been, employed by PACIFIC QUAD, INC., (hereinafter referred to as "PACIFIC QUAD" or "Defendant") in the capacity of operations manager.

2. On or about February 3, YR -2, Plaintiff applied for the position of administrative assistant at PACIFIC QUAD. Schmit interviewed Plaintiff, informed her that she had been hired, and told her to report to work on the following Monday, February 7, YR -2.

3. Plaintiff reported to work at PACIFIC QUAD on February 7, YR -2, and worked there until the middle of the day on February 11, YR -2.

4. During the interview on February 3, YR -2, and throughout the week that Plaintiff worked at PACIFIC QUAD, Plaintiff's immediate supervisor, operations manager Stanley Schmit, subjected Plaintiff to repeated verbal sexual harassment, including, but not limited to, comments directed at various parts of both Plaintiff's and Schmit's anatomy.

5. Throughout the week that Plaintiff worked at PACIFIC QUAD, Schmit subjected Plaintiff to repeated physical sexual harassment, including, but not limited to, unwanted and unsolicited touching.

6. During the interview on February 3, YR -2, and throughout the week that Plaintiff worked at PACIFIC QUAD, Schmit subjected Plaintiff to repeated visual sexual harassment, including, but not limited to, leers of a sexual nature.

7. On or about February 11, YR -2, operations manager Schmit made an unsolicited and unwanted sexual advance toward Plaintiff. Plaintiff rejected Schmit's proposition.

8. On or about the same day, February 11, YR -2, both Schmit and Schmit's supervisor, the president of PACIFIC QUAD, John Walsh, conditioned Plaintiff's continued employment upon her toleration of Schmit's verbal and physical sexual harassment and upon her consenting to Schmit's sexual demands. Walsh further informed Plaintiff that she could "leave" if she was not "happy" with her job. Thus, Walsh made accession to Schmit's sexual demands an implied condition of Plaintiff's employment.

9. On or about February 11, YR -2, Plaintiff was constructively terminated by Defendant in retaliation for her refusal to consent to operations manager Schmit's sexual demands.

10. Defendant's sexual harassment of Plaintiff constitutes sex discrimination and sexual harassment in employment, an unlawful employment practice in violation of the Fair Employment and Housing Act of the State of Nita, Nita Government Code Section 12940(i).

11. Defendant's termination of Plaintiff constitutes sex discrimination and sexual harassment in employment, an unlawful practice in violation of the Fair Employment and Housing Act of the State of Nita, Nita Government Code Section 12940(i).

12. Defendant's conduct in harassing and terminating Plaintiff was intentional, oppressive, and malicious, and was carried out by a managing agent of the corporation.

13. On or about March 23, YR -2, Plaintiff filed a verified complaint with the Department of Fair Employment and Housing of the State of Nita ("DFEH") and the Equal Employment Opportunity

Commission alleging that she had been sexually harassed and terminated by Defendant PACIFIC QUAD.

14. On or about September 12, YR -2, Plaintiff received from the DFEH a notice of her right to bring suit in this action.

15. As a result of Defendant's unlawful employment practices, Plaintiff has suffered lost wages and employment benefits in an amount that has not yet been determined.

16. As a result of Defendant's unlawful employment practices, Plaintiff has incurred expenses for personal and career counseling in an amount that has not yet been determined.

17. As a result of Defendant's unlawful employment practices, Plaintiff has suffered humiliation, embarrassment, and severe emotional stress.

18. As a result of Defendant's unlawful employment practices, Plaintiff has suffered from insomnia, depression, and nightmares.

WHEREFORE Plaintiff prays judgment against Defendant:

1) For back pay in an amount to be determined at trial;

2) For special damages in an amount to be determined at trial;

3) For general damages in an amount to be determined at trial;

4) For exemplary or punitive damages in an amount to be determined at trial; and

5) For such other and further relief as may seem proper to this Court.

DATE: November 3, YR -2

Respectfully submitted,

BENJAMIN J. COHEN,

Attorney for Plaintiff
1341 Haven Court
Nita City, Nita 99990
(721) 555-0479

RETURN OF SUMMONS

I hereby certify that the above Complaint and Summons were personally served on Henry Glenn on the 4th day of November, YR -2.

_____

Process Server

IN THE SUPERIOR COURT OF DARROW COUNTY, NITA

CIVIL DIVISION

ALICE ROWE Plaintiff v. PACIFIC QUAD, INC., Defendant.	)))))))))))))))	Civ. No. O-9876543 NOTICE OF MOTION, MOTION TO DISMISS, AND MOTION TO STRIKE PLAINTIFF'S PRAYERS FOR COMPENSATORY AND EXEMPLARY RELIEF

To ALICE ROWE, Plaintiff, and BENJAMIN J. COHEN, her attorney of record:

Please take notice that on December 15, YR -2, at the hour of 9:30 a.m., or as soon thereafter as counsel can be heard, in Department Fourteen of the Superior Court of the State of Nita, in the City of Nita and County of Darrow, Counsel for the Defendant will move to dismiss Plaintiff's complaint on the ground that it fails to state a claim upon which relief can be granted.

DATE: November 21, YR -2

Henry Glenn
_____

HENRY GLENN

Attorneys for Defendant
Glenn & O'Malley
100 Zee Street, Suite 801
Nita City, Nita 99990
(721) 555-1771

CERTIFICATE OF SERVICE

I hereby certify that on November 21, YR -2, a copy of the above Motions was placed in the United States mail, postage pre-paid, addressed to Benjamin Cohen, 1341 Haven Court, Nita City, Nita.

Barbara Phillips

Barbara Phillips
Glenn & O'Malley
100 Zee Street, Suite 801
Nita City, Nita 99990

PROCEEDINGS OF THE SUPERIOR COURT AND THE COURT OF APPEALS

1. By an Order dated December 15, YR -2, the Superior Court granted Defendant's Motion to Dismiss. The Plaintiff did not amend her Complaint and the Superior Court entered a Judgment of Dismissal on January 17, YR -1.

2. Plaintiff appealed the Superior Court's Judgment of Dismissal to the Nita Court of Appeals. On April 25, YR -1, the Court of Appeals issued an Opinion reversing the Judgment of Dismissal by the Superior Court, and the case was remanded to the trial court for further proceedings. The Court of Appeals opinion is reproduced on pages 87–96 herein.

IN THE SUPERIOR COURT OF DARROW COUNTY, NITA

CIVIL DIVISION

ALICE ROWE   )
Plaintiff   )
)   Civ. No. O-9876543
vs.   )
)   ANSWER
PACIFIC QUAD, INC.,   )
Defendant.   )

Defendant for its answer to the complaint on file herein, admits and denies as follows:

1. Defendant admits the allegations contained in the following paragraphs of Plaintiff's complaint, which are numbered 1, 2, and 3.

2. Defendant denies each and every allegation contained in the following paragraphs of Plaintiff's complaint, which are numbered 4, 5, 6, 7, 8, 9, 10, 11, 15, 16, 17, and 18.

3. Defendant has insufficient knowledge or information to form a belief as to the truth of the allegations set forth in the paragraphs numbered 12, 13, and 14 of Plaintiff's complaint, and on that basis denies the allegations.

WHEREFORE, Defendant prays that Plaintiff take nothing by her said complaint.

DATE: May 9, YR -1

NATIONAL INSTITUTE FOR TRIAL ADVOCACY

Respectfully submitted,

HENRY GLENN

Attorney for Defendant
Glenn & O'Malley
100 Zee Street, Suite 801
Nita City, Nita 99990
(721) 555-1771

CERTIFICATE OF SERVICE

I hereby certify that on May 9, YR -1, a copy of the above Answer was placed in the United States mail, postage prepaid, addressed to Benjamin Cohen, 1341 Haven Court, Nita City, Nita 99990.

Barbara Phillips

Barbara Phillips

Glenn & O'Malley
100 Zee Street, Suite 801
Nita City, Nita 99990

DEPOSITION OF ALICE ROWE*
JULY 14, YR -1

1   My name is Alice Rowe. I live at 1040 Redwood Lane, Nita City, Nita. I have lived in Nita City
2 my whole life. I am twenty-seven years old. I am single.

3   After I graduated from high school, I started going to Nita State University. That was in the fall of
4 YR -10. After three semesters, I think it was, I took some time off from school and got a job as a secre-
5 tary. I did that partly because I needed the money and partly because I just didn't feel right at school.
6 I didn't know what I wanted to major in, or anything, so it seemed like a good idea to do something
7 else for a while.

8   The first job lasted for about six months, then I got a better job as an administrative assistant in a
9 technology company. After a couple of months there, I thought I should try to take some classes about
10 computer science, because it seemed like an interesting subject.

11   I went back to school at Nita State in the spring of YR -7. Everything went fine that semester. I
12 took some computer science classes and did pretty well in them. The next fall wasn't as good, though.
13 I ended up with very boring classes, and I was running out of money again, so in January YR -6 I got
14 another job as an administrative assistant in a software company.

15   I stayed at that job until August YR -6, but then I got laid off because the company was losing
16 money. It was too late then to go back to school for that semester, so I got another admin assistant job,
17 which I kept until July YR -5.

18   By then I was determined to go back to school to finish my degree. I needed four more semesters
19 of work to earn a bachelor of science degree in computer science.

20   That fall semester in YR -5 started off pretty well, but I had problems in one of my classes. I fin-
21 ished out that semester, and I decided to get a job again. I worked as an administrative assistant from
22 January YR -4 through August YR -4. I went back to school and had an easy semester that fall.

23   I had been working as a program assistant during the spring and summer of YR -3, and I had
24 completed the fall semester of YR -3 at school when I applied for the job at Pacific Quad. I would have
25 liked to have stayed at school and finished my degree in the spring of YR -2, but I went to work instead
26 because I needed the money.

27   At some point, I don't really remember when, I was having some problems, and someone suggested
28 that I go see a counselor at the Women's Center at Nita State. That was when I started seeing Anna
29 Mills.

---

*   The transcript of Alice Rowe's deposition was excerpted so that only her answers are reprinted here. Assume that this
     is a true and accurate rendering of those answers.

1   I saw the ad for the job at Pacific Quad at the beginning of the week before I actually started work-
2 ing there. I think that was on Tuesday. I called the phone number in the ad, and they told me to come
3 in and fill out an application. I went in that same afternoon. An administrative assistant gave me an ap-
4 plication form to fill out—the standard questions about skills, experience, and education. I didn't talk
5 to anyone else there that day. Somebody called me the next day—I think it was the same woman—and
6 we arranged for me to come in for an interview on Thursday, February 3, YR -2.

7   The interview took place in the middle of the morning, I think. Around 10:30 I was introduced
8 to Mr. Schmit, and he took me into his office with him and shut the door behind him. I was a little
9 nervous at first—I had had a lot of expenses recently, and I knew that I had to find a job pretty soon.
10 Besides, I think people are always a little nervous in interviews.

11   At first the interview seemed pretty run-of-the-mill. He asked me the usual questions about my
12 prior jobs and talked about what they were looking for. After a couple of minutes, though, the way he
13 was looking at me started to make me feel uncomfortable. At the time, I couldn't have explained what
14 was wrong, but now, on reflection, I feel he was leering at me, staring at my breasts. After a few min-
15 utes, he got up and came around to the side of the desk where I was sitting. We kept talking, mostly
16 about computers, while he paced around, not too far from me. Then he told me that he liked me and
17 would call me later that afternoon about the job. He called me in the middle of the afternoon and of-
18 fered me the job. He said something like, "I can really see us working very closely together. Don't you
19 think so?"

20   I had a funny feeling about Mr. Schmit, but at that point there really wasn't anything definite that
21 I could put my finger on, so I decided to take the job. After all, I thought, first impressions turn out
22 wrong a lot of the time, and it wasn't really that I felt bad about my interview with him—sort of uneasy
23 would be more like it.

24   I reported to work the next Monday morning. Mr. Schmit showed me where my desk was and
25 introduced me to the people in the offices. The two other administrative assistants and I worked in a
26 large open area in the middle of the office. A four-foot high partition wall divided up the area into four
27 cubicles. We each had one cubicle, with a desk and a computer. The fourth cubicle was used for files.

28   The front doors of the office were in the middle of one wall near the other two assistants. There
29 were offices and a lunchroom along the other three walls. Mr. Schmit's office was the closest to my
30 desk. The door to his office was about ten feet away from my desk. When he was sitting at his desk,
31 he could see me working at my computer if he leaned forward a little. As a matter of fact, a couple of
32 times that week, when I was entering data, I got the feeling that someone was looking at me, and when
33 I turned around, I thought I saw him leaning back away from the door, as if he had been watching me
34 but didn't want me to see that he had been looking.

35   At the beginning of that week I stayed very busy, and I didn't really have time to pay much atten-
36 tion to Mr. Schmit. My job was supposed to be to take care of correspondence and sales data entry,
37 and there was a lot to learn and a lot of work piled up for me. I spent most of Monday morning reading
38 some of the incoming e-mail that I was supposed to answer and reading through the canned answers,
39 so that I could get a feeling for what I was supposed to do.

1   Mr. Schmit came by my desk a few times on Monday or Tuesday and talked to me. I don't really
2 remember exactly what he said. I think it was just "How's it going?" or "Got any questions?" The thing
3 that stuck out in my mind, though, even on the first day, was the way he looked at me. Just like in the
4 interview, he wasn't exactly staring at me, but something in the way he looked at me always gave me
5 the chills. In a way it was as if he was sizing me up, from head to toe. Sometimes when I happened to
6 look in his direction, it seemed like he was leering at my breasts. It was really impersonal—he never
7 looked me in the eye when he had been looking at me that way, but he also didn't look away or seem
8 embarrassed. He just kept looking.

9   The first few days I kept trying to ignore Mr. Schmit. I really was busy, and I didn't want to start
10 off my new job by having problems with the boss, so I just told myself not to be silly, that I was imag-
11 ining things, that everything was fine.

12   After lunch on Tuesday or Wednesday, though, things got worse. Mr. Schmit asked me if I had
13 enjoyed my lunch, and then he said something like, "I really enjoy eating out." I didn't think anything
14 of it, until I heard him chuckle, and when I looked at him, I saw that he had this big grin on his face,
15 and he gave me a big wink. Then I felt my face get warm, and I didn't really know what to do or say,
16 so I just went and sat at my desk and stared at the computer screen.

17   Later that afternoon, Mr. Schmit was standing in his doorway talking to some of the other em-
18 ployees. I don't really remember who else was there, but they were joking around. Mr. Schmit told a
19 few dirty jokes. I don't really remember exactly what they were, but one of them had to do with women
20 with large breasts.

21   One morning I got to work a few minutes before he did. I was just settling in at my desk when he
22 came up behind me to say something about how nice I looked that day. I guess I must have really been
23 edgy, because he startled me when he said that, and I jumped a little bit. When he saw me jump, he
24 laughed, put his hand on my shoulder, and said something like, "There, there, I'm not really that scary,
25 am I?" I don't think I said anything then, and he walked away.

26   That day just seemed to get worse and worse. He kept looking at me in the same way. It seemed
27 as if he spent most of that day joking around with different people somewhere near my desk, and his
28 sense of humor seemed to focus pretty much on sex and double meanings. I can't remember exactly the
29 words he used, but they were talking about computers, and he kept talking about them "going down"
30 and "coming up," and then everyone would nudge each other and laugh. Even when he wasn't talking
31 directly to me like that, I was offended by a lot of what he said. It seemed that it was just normal for
32 him to talk the way I suppose men do in locker rooms—just vulgar most of the time.

33   Right at the end of the day, Mr. Schmit came up to my desk and started talking with me. He
34 looked at the papers on my desk, and he said, "Looks like you're getting a little behind in your work.
35 I'd sure like to get a little behind in mine." I blushed, and he gave me a wink as he walked back into
36 his office. Fortunately it was time for me to go home when he said that, because I was really upset.

37   All that night I kept thinking about what was going on, and I doubt that I slept at all. I knew that
38 I wasn't just making things up at that point, and I really didn't know what to do. I wanted to talk to
39 someone at work about it, but there really wasn't anyone that I felt I could talk to. I thought about

1 talking to Mr. Walsh, because he was Mr. Schmit's boss, but I had barely met him, and he didn't seem
2 like someone who would be easy to talk to.

3 Another thing that Mr. Schmit had been doing was touching me "accidentally." If we were passing
4 by each other, he always brushed into me, even though there was always enough room for him to get by
5 me without touching me. The worst time was on Thursday, when he walked behind me and brushed
6 his hand against my behind. It didn't feel like an accident; I must have jumped ten feet. I said, "Don't
7 do that!" He just laughed, and said, "Do what?"

8 Friday morning I was there for about an hour before he got there. When he got to the office, he
9 stopped at my desk on the way to his office. He smiled and said something like, "Well, Alice, you sure
10 look good today." I didn't say a word, but I didn't like it.

11 About an hour later, he leaned forward over his desk and called me into his office. I just can't re-
12 member his exact words, but he asked me to go out with him over the weekend. I said something like,
13 "No, I don't think so," and asked why. He had a big grin and winked at me and said, "It's business."
14 I asked him what business had to do with us going out on the weekend, and he said, "We'll see what
15 comes up." When he said that, I knew he meant it as a sexual proposition.

16 I walked out of his office and was sitting at my desk, shaking, trying to figure out what to do, when
17 he came out of the office to my desk and started to talk to me. Suddenly I realized that I just couldn't
18 take any more of it, and I told him that I wasn't going to play his games anymore. I got up and went
19 out in the hall to take a deep breath. I started crying, so I went into the ladies' room.

20 After I had calmed down, I decided to go tell Mr. Walsh what was going on. I walked into his
21 office and explained what had been going on all week. It's true that I was upset, but he must have
22 understood what I was saying. He just didn't want to be bothered, he said, and then he said, "If you're
23 not happy with the job, you can leave."

24 At that point I didn't think I had any choice. Mr. Schmit wasn't going to stop, and Mr. Walsh
25 didn't care. I felt completely helpless and frustrated. I walked to my desk, got my purse, told Mr.
26 Schmit "I'm quitting," and left.

27 All of that was more than a year ago, but it still upsets me to talk or think about it. For a long time,
28 I felt so used by them. It was all that I thought about for months. I started seeing Anna Mills pretty
29 often so that we could talk about my feelings. She kept trying to tell me that not everyone was out to
30 take advantage of me, but deep down it took a long time before I could believe that.

31 Those first few months I had a hard time sleeping, and when I did fall asleep, I had nightmares
32 about being harassed. Gradually, things got better, and in September of last year I got a job.

33 On September 12, YR -2, I began work as an administrative assistant for Business Systems, Inc.,
34 which is an office supply company. I work for their Director of Purchasing, Ms. Susan Lindbloom,
35 and I started at a salary of $3,500 per month. I received a raise effective January 1, YR -1, to $3,600
36 per month.

37 It was a big relief to be getting a paycheck again, because I had had to borrow money from my
38 parents to get by during the time I wasn't working. I didn't tell them what had happened to me until a
39 couple of months ago, so I don't know what they must have thought was going on before then.

1   One of these days, I'm still planning to go back and get my degree. This whole business has made
2 that a lot more difficult. Obviously, it caused me a lot of mental anguish. I really wasn't able to do
3 anything for a long time. On top of that, it has caused some serious financial hardships for me. I still
4 owe my parents money from the time when I couldn't work. I don't know when I will be able to stop
5 working and go back to school, but I'm still not giving up hope.
6   I filed a charge of sexual harassment once before. It was when I was in school; I don't remember
7 what year it was. I was taking a seminar class, and I noticed that the professor kept staring at me. He
8 made some strange comments—jokes that could have had an innocent meaning but obviously had
9 some sexual double meaning from the way that he and some of the students laughed at them. He
10 always looked at me when he made the jokes. I knew that the other students realized what was going
11 on.
12   At first I was just trying to ignore him, but then I had a meeting with him in his office to discuss
13 the paper I was writing. It's so long ago now that I don't really remember the details of what happened,
14 but I remember that he asked me to go out with him. He acted strange when I said no, and when I tried
15 to talk to him about it later, he pretended that he didn't know what I was talking about. After that he
16 ignored me in class, so finally I decided to file a complaint against him. By then, I was so upset that I
17 had pretty much stopped going to his class.
18   The school had a grievance board for sexual harassment complaints, and there was a hearing on my
19 complaint. Of course, the professor denied everything, but I felt vindicated by the grievance board. As
20 I said, everyone realized what was really going on. I was allowed to drop the course without penalty.
21 The hearing was very embarrassing for the professor, and I'm sure that he never again treated anyone
22 else that way.
23   This deposition was taken in the office of defendant's counsel on July 14, YR -1. This deposition
24 was given under oath and was read and signed by the deponent.

Certified by:

Anne Dolan

Anne Dolan
Certified Shorthand Reporter
(CSR)

BENJAMIN J. COHEN

Attorney at Law
1341 Haven Court
Nita City, Nita 99990
(721) 555-0479

September 11, YR -1

Henry Glenn, Esq.
Glenn & O'Malley
100 Zee Street, Suite 801
Nita City, Nita 99990

RE: Alice Rowe v. Pacific Quad, Inc.

Dear Mr. Glenn:

Alice Rowe has received her deposition and affirms that it is correct, except for the fourth full paragraph on page 22, which should be amended to read as follows:

"I walked out of his office and then sat at my desk, shaking, trying to figure out what to do, when he came out of his office to my desk and started to talk to me. Suddenly I realized that I just couldn't take any more of it, and I told him that I wasn't going to play his games any more. He had a gleam in his eye and responded, 'That's a low blow. And speaking of...'. Without waiting for him to finish, I got up and went out in the hall to take a deep breath. I started crying, so I went into the ladies' room."

Sincerely,

Benjamin J. Cohen

Benjamin J. Cohen

BJC:ak

DEPOSITION OF ANNA MILLS*
AUGUST 17, YR -1

1   My name is Anna Mills. I live at 1909 Pacific Shores Lane, Nita City, Nita.

2   I am a Licensed Clinical Social Worker. I have master's degrees in social work and counseling. I

3   have worked as a counselor at the Women's Center of Nita State University here in Nita City for the

4   past five years. As a counselor in the Women's Center, I function in several different capacities. First,

5   I provide career counseling for our women students and alumnae. I also run discussion sessions and

6   workshops relating to women's issues. I provide individual personal counseling, and I direct a peer

7   counseling program. Further, I do special counseling for victims of rape and sexual harassment. In this

8   last role, I provide crisis intervention and long-term counseling, and I also advise and assist students

9   who wish to seek official redress for the acts committed against them. I have provided all of these ser-

10   vices since assuming my position at the Women's Center.

11   I first met Alice Rowe in the fall of YR -5. I met her when she came to the Women's Center with

12   a complaint against a professor. I helped her file the complaint and counseled her throughout the

13   investigation. Alice is a very intelligent young woman who is now only a semester away from earning

14   her bachelor of science degree in computer science, but she has repeatedly taken time off from school

15   to work at secretarial jobs. In my opinion, this is because of a fear of success and lack of self esteem. In

16   our counseling sessions, Alice and I discussed both pragmatic career planning goals and strategies and

17   her deep-seated fears and doubts, which were manifested in her academic and personal life.

18   Although I generally work only with students from the University, I occasionally continue with

19   counseling sessions after students leave the University. The University requires that non-students pay

20   for these sessions. We use a sliding-scale fee schedule. During the second half of YR -3 and January

21   YR -2, Alice was coming to me for counseling sessions once a week, sometimes once every two weeks.

22   From February YR -2, when the incident at Pacific Quad happened, through October YR -2, Alice

23   came to counseling sessions twice a week, occasionally three times a week. Since then, Alice has been

24   coming to counseling sessions once a week. Since February YR -2, Alice has paid $7,085 (109 sessions

25   at $65 per session) in counseling fees.

26   During February and the months that followed in YR -2, Alice and I discussed extensively the

27   reported incident of sexual harassment at Pacific Quad. Alice told me that she had been propositioned

28   and otherwise pressured sexually by her supervisor at Pacific Quad and then forced to resign when she

29   would not go along with his advances.

---

*   The transcript of Anna Mills's deposition was excerpted so that only her answers are reprinted here. Assume that this
     is a true and accurate rendering of those answers.

1   The perceived harassment had a serious psychological effect on Alice. She could function on a
2   basic level, but she was not sufficiently emotionally stable to return to work for seven months. She had
3   nightmares and insomnia. The trauma, which she felt as a result of the harassment, undid much of the
4   progress she and I had made. She is back at work now, but her educational plans are still unsettled. She
5   still has difficulty establishing trusting, close relationships with men.

6   I have Alice's counseling file with me today. There is nothing in the file relating directly to our
7   counseling sessions, as it is not my practice to take notes during or after the sessions. The only writing
8   in the file other than billing records is a letter concerning Alice that I wrote to a colleague of mine, Saul
9   Jacobs. Saul is a counselor in private practice, and I often ask him to be available for my clients when
10 I go out of town. In the summer of YR -2, I was away at a conference and on vacation for a period of
11 about five weeks, and I asked Saul to fill in for me. When I do this, I sometimes send Saul a description
12 of some of my clients, as a sort of "introduction" to them. I wrote one such memo to Saul concerning
13 Alice. In the letter I briefly described Alice's situation and my psychological assessment. You'd like to
14 copy the memo? I'd assumed Mr. Cohen had already given you a copy. You've never seen it before?
15 OK, here it is.

16 I used some language in the memo that I now regret, as I have been informed that it could be
17 misinterpreted. I never meant to indicate by anything I wrote that I disbelieved Alice's report of sexual
18 harassment at Pacific Quad. I had then, and I have now, full confidence that Alice perceived the situ-
19 ation accurately and reported it to me truthfully.

20 The poor choice of words in my memo should not be taken as imputing Alice's integrity. It was my
21 fault. I guess I was just very busy when I wrote it.

22 This deposition was taken in the office of defendant's counsel on August 17, YR -l. This deposition
23 was given under oath, and was read and signed by the deponent.

Certified by:

Anne Dolan

Anne Dolan
Certified Shorthand Reporter
(CSR)

DEPOSITION OF GLORIA WARNER*
AUGUST 24, YR -1

1   My name is Gloria Warner. I live at 355 Linda Mar Road, Nita City, Nita. I am twenty-eight years
2 old. I graduated from Nita State University with a degree in business administration in YR -6. I am
3 currently employed as a sales person for Orange Computers.

4   I worked as a sales representative for Pacific Quad, Inc., from December YR -4 to August 26,
5 YR -2. John Walsh was my immediate supervisor. When I was at Pacific Quad, I was actually in the
6 office only about one-third to one-half of the time. The rest of the time I was out meeting with clients
7 in their offices.

8   My office at Pacific Quad was right next to Mr. Schmit's office. The walls of the office are pretty
9 thin, so sometimes I could hear conversations in his office when the rest of the office was not too
10 noisy.

11   One day in early February YR -2, I was sitting in my office when I heard Mr. Schmit say to John
12 Walsh, "Hey, I've just hired a real babe as my secretary." I did not hear either one of them specifically
13 mention Alice Rowe's name, but Alice was the only person hired around the time I heard the remark,
14 so I am sure that they were talking about her.

15   I first heard that Alice Rowe had filed a complaint about sexual harassment at the beginning of the
16 summer, a few months after Alice worked at Pacific Quad. Mr. Schmit approached me, waving a piece
17 of paper in his hand, saying, "Remember that hysterical chick, Rowe, you know, the one that was only
18 here for a week? Well, would you look at this garbage—now she thinks that I wanted to go to bed with
19 her—that crazy broad!"

20   I was not fired by Pacific Quad. They had no reason to fire me. I always did my job. I resent that
21 question; I never missed any appointments with clients. I left voluntarily because I wanted to take a
22 break from the pressure. The industry had gotten more competitive in YR -2, so everyone's sales were
23 down. The pressure was a lot more than when I first started working at Pacific Quad. I wanted to work
24 in a less stressful field.

25   Stanley Schmit never asked me to go out with him. He never really said anything to me that was
26 sexual, but there were quite a few times when I got uncomfortable about the way he was looking at me.
27 It was as if he was undressing me with his eyes. I never said anything about it to anyone—what was I
28 supposed to say? Who would I tell it to?

---

*   The transcript of Gloria Warner's deposition was excerpted so that only her answers are reprinted here. Assume that
this is a true and accurate rendering of those answers.

1   This deposition was taken in the office of defendant's counsel on August 24, YR -1. This deposi-

2   tion was given under oath, and was read and signed by the deponent.

Certified by:

Anne Dolan

_____

Anne Dolan
Certified Shorthand Reporter
(CSR)

Deposition of John Walsh*
June 22, YR -1

1   My name is John Walsh. I live at 2767 Goldcoast Circle, Nita Highlands, Nita. I am married with
2   two children, one boy and one girl.

3   I am the president and co-owner of Pacific Quad, Inc. I started the company with two friends,
4   Wilbur Matthews and Jason Novak, in August of YR -4. We all left BMI to start up a company of our
5   own. I am the principal shareholder, and I am responsible for the general operations of the company.
6   I have been principally responsible for all general company business matters since the inception of the
7   company.

8   The main assets of Pacific Quad consist of copyrighted software designed by myself, Wilbur, and
9   Jason. Briefly, Pacific Quad provides consultant services to devise creative solutions to the information
10   management problems of medium-sized businesses. We help businesses increase the ease and efficiency
11   with which they use their technology systems.

12   Usually the sales representatives locate clients and get a basic understanding of the problems that
13   the clients are experiencing. Then I work closely with the clients and the salespeople in analyzing the
14   problems and developing solutions. Generally, we will sell the clients a package of software to meet
15   their needs, including our own software custom-designed by Wilbur, Jason, or me. Additionally, we
16   will advise clients regarding any necessary hardware they will need to purchase, although we neither
17   make nor sell hardware. In sum, we like to think of ourselves as creative problem solvers rather than
18   mere software salespeople. Needless to say, I work very closely with the sales representatives.

19   Pacific Quad currently employs twelve people, and has been profitable since YR -3. In YR -2 Pacific
20   Quad paid $700,000 in salary to myself, $350,000 each in consulting fees to Matthews and Novak,
21   and $55,000 in salary to Stanley Schmit. Our net profit after taxes was $850,000. No figures are yet
22   available for YR -1, but so far it has been a good year. I would estimate that a good salesperson at Pacific
23   Quad would earn between $100,000 and $150,000 per year.

24   From the beginning, the whole concept of this company has been on the model of a small, friendly,
25   and cooperative office. We have all become like a family. Even though we have grown in size some-
26   what, we remain, after four years, a company of only twelve employees. Everything that happens here
27   I take personally. Thus, I am personally disturbed about Ms. Rowe's accusations of sexual harassment
28   and find this whole matter quite disruptive to the harmony that has characterized our office from the
29   very start.

---

*   The transcript of John Walsh's deposition was excerpted so that only his answers are reprinted here. Assume that this
    is a true and accurate rendering of those answers.

1   Yes, we do have an anti-harassment policy. It's oral. I've instructed Stanley Schmit to explain to
2 every new employee that we will not tolerate harassment or discrimination of any kind. Also, Stanley
3 and I have taken an on-line sexual harassment training course for managers. I don't remember it very
4 well, but I certainly didn't learn anything from it I didn't already know. The point of it was to empha-
5 size that we should always treat employees with respect; that's something we all do here.

6   I still cannot fathom what Ms. Rowe is complaining about. All I know is that she worked for us
7 for one week, from Monday, February 7, YR -2, to Friday, February 11, YR -2. Ms. Rowe began work
8 on Monday and worked all the week through until just before lunchtime on Friday. She seemed nice
9 enough when I met her, but I really didn't pay much attention to her day-to-day activities. That's
10 Stanley's job. He's in charge of making new employees feel at home in the office—helping them to
11 become familiar with office procedure and the work they will be doing. As our operations manager,
12 Stanley is the one who makes sure that the ship sails smoothly—that the bills get paid, that the ac-
13 counts receivable are collected, that correspondence goes out, and that everyone gets along. Stanley is
14 kind of my "guy Friday."

15   On Friday, February 11, I was sitting in my office around noontime, and Ms. Rowe came in. She
16 seemed very upset. Her eyes were very wet and red, and it looked as if she had been crying. She began
17 mumbling and sobbing at the same time, so I couldn't understand everything she was trying to say.
18 But she seemed to be saying something about men, about her not being able to get along with men. I
19 think she said, "This always happens to me." I was somewhat taken aback, really confused about her
20 remarks, but after a while she calmed down a little. I asked if there was anything I could do to help
21 her, and I suggested she might want to leave for a break. I thought that perhaps some fresh air might
22 help her, and it was time for a lunch break anyway. After I made that suggestion, she got up and left,
23 but she never came back.

24   When I didn't see Ms. Rowe at her desk that afternoon, I asked Stanley Schmit about her. Mr.
25 Schmit informed me that she had quit without giving any reason. He told me that he thought that
26 maybe she had some personal problems and just couldn't handle the job, because she had been agitated
27 all week long.

28   I don't know where Ms. Rowe got the idea that there was any sexual harassment. She really has an
29 overactive imagination. I have talked to Mr. Schmit, and I am certain that he never sexually harassed
30 Ms. Rowe. I know Stanley Schmit never intended to offend or embarrass anyone. He also never propo-
31 sitioned Ms. Rowe or asked her out on a date. Mr. Schmit's job is to make employees feel comfortable
32 with their work, and no one has ever complained about his work relations before. Everyone at the office
33 gets along fine, thanks to Stanley Schmit.

34   Gloria Warner worked for Pacific Quad from December YR -4 until August 26, YR -2. Gloria
35 worked as a sales representative. Although we liked her, her work was just not up to our standards. She
36 kept missing appointments with clients, and we finally had to let her go. We do not have any written
37 proof of her unsatisfactory work performance—that is not the way we operate. As I said before, we are
38 a small business and we deal with each other on an informal basis.

39   Now it seems that Gloria is bitter enough about her own situation with Pacific Quad to try to get
40 back at us. But there was nothing we could do about not keeping her on. I thought she realized that,

1 and cared about what was good for the company. I even gave her a good recommendation—I'm not a
2 vindictive person.
3   This deposition was taken in the office of plaintiff's counsel on June 22, YR -1. This deposition
4 was given under oath and was read and signed by the deponent.

Certified by:

Roger Powell
_____

Roger Powell
Certified Shorthand Reporter
(CSR)

DEPOSITION OF STANLEY SCHMIT*
JULY 20, YR -1

1   My name is Stanley James Schmit. I live at 3215 Bonnet Shores Drive, Nita City, Nita. I am thirty-
2   two years old. I am married to Annie Jane Schmit, formerly Annie Jane Lee. We have been happily
3   married for three years. We have one son who turned one year old in April. My wife Annie does not
4   work. She stays home with Stan Jr., our son.

5   I work at Pacific Quad, Inc. I have been working for Pacific Quad since the company got started.
6   At that time the company was much smaller than it is now. There were only a few of us in the com-
7   pany, plus a few secretaries. We've all worked really hard to build this company, and I feel like I know
8   every facet of the business since I've been with it right from the start. When we first started up, I was
9   the only sales representative in the whole outfit. About a year after we had been in business, in January
10   of YR -3, I was promoted to operations manager. I have held that position ever since.

11   The president of the company is Mr. John Walsh. Mr. Walsh has two other partners, Mr. Wilbur
12   Matthews and Mr. Jason Novak, but they do not come into the office very often. They have their own
13   computer systems at home. They do not have responsibility for the daily operations of the company.
14   Mr. Walsh is really the only other management person besides myself who is in the office on a daily
15   basis. But even though he's here in the office, I'm the one who runs the day-to-day operations of the
16   company.

17   As operations manager I have to be on top of whatever comes into the office. I sit down with Mr.
18   Walsh, and we talk about the marketing situation, our sales goals, and all the other things that make
19   up this business. Of course, Mr. Walsh makes the decisions regarding the long-range aspects of the
20   business, but I handle the daily problems that come up in the office. I supervise the employees at Pa-
21   cific Quad. Well, not all of the employees, the sales staff are directly responsible to Mr. Walsh. But I
22   supervise the office staff—the secretaries and the bookkeeper. I am also responsible for hiring and fir-
23   ing employees. Well, I've never actually fired anyone, but if I had to, I'm sure Mr. Walsh would approve
24   my decision. I do take care of the hiring, though. That is, I take care of all the details of the process.

25   In order to hire a new employee, I either put an ad on craigslist, or list the job with an employment
26   agency. Applicants come in and fill out a regular application form, and then we decide who to call back
27   for an interview. The application asks about standard things, like biographical data, any work experi-
28   ence, and references. Since we're a high-tech firm, we look for prior experience with technology. That's
29   critical. Also, for secretaries, they need to know all the Microsoft Office programs.

---

*   The transcript of Stanley Schmit's deposition was excerpted so that only his answers are reprinted here. Assume that
    this is a correct and accurate rendering of those answers.

1   I look over the applications after they're filled out, and I usually pick the ones I think should be
2 called back for an interview. Then I give my recommendations to Mr. Walsh, and he makes the final
3 decision. I get my secretary to call the girls up and set up interviews. I usually do the interviews, and I
4 usually have one of the girls in the office sit in. We're a small company, and it's important that everyone
5 gets along. So even though I ask the questions, I like to have one of the secretaries there to make sure
6 everyone will be able to work together.

7   We only keep interviewing applicants until we find someone we like, and then we call them up and
8 hire them. I generally figure out who's right for the job, and then Mr. Walsh gives the final go-ahead.
9 But really it's an office decision, not a top-down decision. I give folks in the office a chance to say what
10 they think and then decide based on all factors put together. If there's a general feeling that the girl
11 won't work out, there's no point in hiring her. Mr. Walsh feels the same way. Aside from Alice Rowe,
12 we have hired about two or three other secretaries since I became operations manager in YR -3.

13   We decided to hire another secretary because the company was growing. At the time we made the
14 decision to hire, we were down to two secretaries. Since becoming operations manager, I had noticed
15 that the e-mail correspondence had been mounting up, and I thought that we would be more efficient
16 if just one secretary took care of all of the e-mail inquiries. That way she would know where to send
17 everything without going through the records each time. I discussed the idea with Mr. Walsh several
18 times at the end of YR -3, but we didn't get around to advertising for the position until February 1,
19 YR -2.

20   We had about six or seven qualified applicants for the position. We actually interviewed about two
21 other applicants before Alice Rowe. Ms. Rowe came in for an interview on the morning of February 3,
22 YR -2. After interviewing Ms. Rowe, we stopped interviewing candidates and hired her for the job. She
23 was the candidate with the most relevant experience because she had worked for a technology company
24 before. The other applicants all had less experience.

25   I don't recall the interview with Ms. Rowe in too much detail, but I remember being very im-
26 pressed with her background. I conducted the interview by myself. The interview took place in my
27 office, which is private. Because the door to the office was closed during the interview, there were no
28 distractions or disturbances from the general office activity going on at the time. I like to conduct in-
29 terviews without distractions. It allows me to concentrate on getting to know the person and figuring
30 out whether they will fit in and be able to do the job.

31   Ms. Rowe seemed really nervous during the interview. It wasn't just normal interview nerves; I
32 would have to describe her behavior as "jumpy." Her tone of voice was defensive. Her responses to
33 my questions were short and quick, and she talked very fast. It seemed as if she was being tested or
34 something. She kept fidgeting, too, and looking around the room and shifting her weight from side
35 to side.

36   I hired Ms. Rowe the afternoon of the interview. I did not talk to anyone about my decision but
37 just went ahead and offered her the job. I had spoken with Mr. Walsh about her sometime after she
38 filed her application, and we were both very impressed with her past experience.

39   The interview took place on February 3, a Thursday. Ms. Rowe was to begin work on Monday,
40 February 7.

1   That Monday I arrived at work as usual. Although I don't remember the exact time, it must have
2   been somewhere between 7:30 and 8:00. Probably around 7:45 a.m. Ms. Rowe arrived at work around
3   8:00. I started her off by introducing her to the people that were in the office. We really don't have a
4   formal orientation process because we have virtually no employee turnover. I recall that not everyone
5   was there. Some of the salesmen were out of the office. But I think Gloria Warner and Sam Frigate
6   were there. Also Joe, our shipping clerk, and Joyce, our bookkeeper. Mr. Walsh was there as well. After
7   introductions, I showed Alice where she would sit and where everything was—the files, the supplies,
8   the ladies' room.

9   I remember that on her first morning at work, Ms. Rowe seemed just as nervous and fidgety as she
10   had been during the interview. She kept playing with her hair—running her fingers through it and
11   twisting it. She also kept looking away from me or around the room as I was talking to her, as if she
12   wasn't concentrating. It was as if she was afraid of something or worried that something would happen
13   to her. I didn't think much about it after a while. I just thought she was like that, because she kept
14   acting nervous and preoccupied. She never changed. She kept acting like that the whole week she was
15   there.

16   That week I talked to Ms. Rowe a number of times, to give her assignments and check up on what
17   she was doing. I had to make a point to go over and talk to her because her desk is out in the large
18   front office, along with the other secretaries. My desk is in my office along the back wall, and I wasn't
19   able to just converse with Ms. Rowe while I was at my desk. To tell you the truth, the way our desks
20   are situated, in order to even see Ms. Rowe's desk my door would have to be open and I'd have to lean
21   across the side of my desk. That's the only way I can get a pretty good view of the whole office.

22   I often pass by the secretaries in order to find out how they're doing with their work. That's part of
23   my job as operations manager. I have to make sure everything is running smoothly in the office. I also
24   have to make sure everyone is getting along and not fighting with one another. We are a small office,
25   and we are always friendly and kidding with each other. It's very much like a family situation. I try to
26   make everyone smile, and many times I will compliment the girls.

27   No one has ever complained about my comments before. In fact, everyone in the office got along
28   just fine before Ms. Rowe came along. It's such a small, close-knit group of people. We're always tell-
29   ing the girls when they've done a good job. It makes them feel more a part of things. We do the same
30   with the salesmen.

31   I tried to make Ms. Rowe feel more at ease. It's part of my job to make sure people in the office are
32   happy. I even remember telling Ms. Rowe that her dress was nice on one occasion. And I might even
33   have made a comment to one of the other girls that I thought Ms. Rowe was good-looking. But if I did,
34   I certainly didn't mean any harm by it. I just wanted her to feel more at home with the company.

35   As for saying anything about sex, I never talk to my secretaries about sexual intercourse, or sexual
36   organs, or any such things. I have a lot of respect for my girls. Of course, we tell jokes to each other;
37   there's a lot of laughing in the office, but it's just kidding around. And everybody does it. That is, of
38   course, everybody but Ms. Rowe. When I think back on it now, she really didn't have much of a sense
39   of humor. She just acted nervous and kept to herself. She was really pretty unfriendly. It didn't matter

1 whether I talked to her in private in my office or out on the floor in front of the other girls. She always
2 acted the same.

3 But I never said anything sexual to Ms. Rowe. And I certainly never propositioned her. I never
4 said any such things on Friday, February 11, and I never said any such things on any other day Ms.
5 Rowe came to work. During that whole week, I never even asked Ms. Rowe about her private life. I
6 don't even know if she has a boyfriend or not, though I doubt it. I never asked her about that, or who
7 she was sleeping with, or anything like that. The most I got personal with her was to maybe tell her
8 that her dress looked nice. It's hardly anything to get all worked up about. I thought she would like
9 the compliment.

10 I certainly never physically touched Ms. Rowe, ever. Come to think of it, I don't even think I shook
11 her hand when she came in for the interview.

12 Ms. Rowe kept on working for the whole week. Her work was OK, but she really did seem nervous.
13 Nothing I did to try to be friendly made it any better. Finally, on Friday, February 11, she just walked
14 out of the office without any explanation to me at all and never came back. Right before she left, I had
15 gone up to her desk to see how she was doing. I was on my way out to lunch. I was trying to be friendly
16 so I said something like, "How's everything going?" I think I might have joked about giving her too
17 much work, just to make conversation and loosen things up. She mumbled something in return.

18 Then Ms. Rowe got up from her desk and mumbled something under her breath. But it wasn't
19 anything like she claims, "I don't have to put up with this—I'm not going to play your games." That
20 wouldn't have made any sense. I would have asked her to explain it if she said that. I really didn't know
21 what she was talking about when she got up. I thought she just got up to go to the bathroom.

22 A few minutes later after she got up, I saw her coming out of Mr. Walsh's office. She said, "I'm quit-
23 ting," picked up her purse, and walked out. It was very bizarre. I didn't know what to think, whether
24 she was quitting or just being weird as usual. Before I had a chance to ask her, she had already walked
25 out. It all happened really fast.

26 When I came back from lunch, Mr. Walsh asked me about the incident. I told him I didn't have
27 any idea what was going on, but that I guessed she just wasn't happy or had some personal problems or
28 something. Next thing I know, John Walsh is telling me that Ms. Rowe quit her job because she claims
29 I asked her out and she didn't want to go. I was speechless. I never asked Ms. Rowe out on a date. I
30 never even asked her out to lunch. I certainly never asked her out for a drink or to spend any time
31 with me outside the office. I do remember saying something to her like "I hope we can get together
32 sometime," but I certainly didn't mean that I wanted to go out on a date with her. I was just trying to
33 be friendly with her. She was always so nervous. I really didn't find her all that attractive, so I wouldn't
34 be trying to go out with her. After all, I'm married with a one-year-old son.

35 That's all I can remember about Ms. Rowe. She was only there for one week, and as far as I knew
36 until she started up this trouble, she was a strange kind of girl who didn't get along in the office. I guess
37 I'm not surprised she quit. She just didn't fit into the office group. But I certainly didn't have anything
38 to do with her problems. As far as I knew, she had them before she came. Even now, I still don't know
39 what she's complaining about. It's all simply untrue.

1   Yes, we do have a sexual harassment policy. Our policy is that we don't permit it. No, it's not writ-
2 ten or posted, but everyone who works here should know about it. If Alice Rowe had a complaint, she
3 could have brought it right to me or to Mr. Walsh.

4   I took an on-line sexual harassment training course a few years ago. It was pretty interesting. It was
5 mostly about girls harassing guys or harassing other girls, and girls telling racy stories. I was surprised
6 to learn that that's sexual harassment. It also covered guys hitting on girls. It said you're not supposed
7 to do that at work. That was pretty much it.

8   This deposition was taken in the office of plaintiff's counsel on July 20, YR -1. This deposition was
9 given under oath and was read and signed by the deponent.

Certified by:

Roger Powell

_____

Roger Powell
Certified Shorthand Reporter
(CSR)

Glenn & O'Malley

Attorneys at Law
100 Zee Street, Suite 801
Nita City, Nita 99990
(721) 555-1771

September 22, YR -1

Benjamin J. Cohen
Attorney at Law
1341 Haven Court
Nita City, Nita 99990

RE: Alice Rowe v. Pacific Quad, Inc.

Dear Mr. Cohen:

Stanley Schmit has read his deposition and affirms that it is correct, except for the following corrections:

1. The following should be inserted as the third full paragraph on page 37 at line 16:

"I began to notice by the middle of the week that Ms. Rowe's performance was less than satisfactory. Her typing speed was much slower than her resume indicated, and her pace of work in general was slow. Further, she often seemed distracted or uninterested when I gave her assignments and discussed her work with her. I had discussed this with Mr. Walsh late Thursday afternoon, and we were considering letting Ms. Rowe go if her performance did not improve."

2. The second sentence of the third full paragraph on page 38 at line 12 should read in its entirety, "She really did seem nervous."

Henry Glenn

Henry Glenn

HG:lws

Henry Glenn • Julia Johnson • Thomas Doyle • Dorothy Levee • Dennis Bernards
Joseph Doyle II – Of Counsel

DEPOSITION OF SUSAN ROBINSON*
JULY 27, YR -1

1   My name is Susan Robinson. I am twenty-seven years old and single. I live at 357 Bonnet Court,
2 Nita City, Nita. I have lived in Nita all my life.

3   I currently work as a secretary for Pacific Quad, Inc. I have been working at Pacific Quad since
4 February 16, YR -2. I went to work there because I heard that the company needed a new adminis-
5 trative assistant. I learned of this from Stanley Schmit, my current supervisor. Stanley is a very close
6 friend of my brother's from their college days, and I have known him for many years. When he told
7 me that Pacific Quad just lost their new assistant, I went right over for the job. I had been working
8 as an assistant since YR -6, but I was looking for a higher paying job at the time. I started work right
9 after that interview.

10   During my years as an administrative assistant, I have worked in a variety of offices and businesses.
11 I have worked for many executives and have had to work closely with many of them. From all this
12 experience, I can attest to the good character of Stanley Schmit. Stanley has always treated me with
13 the greatest respect and courtesy. He has always acted in a highly professional manner and is a model
14 of gentlemanly behavior.

15   I have never heard Mr. Schmit tease or ridicule anyone in a sexually offensive manner. I can't re-
16 member too many occasions when he has actually used sexually explicit language, and even when he
17 has used such language on rare occasions, it has certainly not been offensive. In all the time I have been
18 at Pacific Quad, I have never seen him conduct himself in any way that would even remotely suggest
19 sexual harassment. He has never made any sexual advances of any kind toward me, and I have never
20 seen him do anything like that toward anyone else in the office. I am somewhat shocked to learn of
21 this false accusation. I'm sure he will be vindicated in this matter.

22   Although I did not meet Ms. Rowe, since I came to work at Pacific Quad after she left, I can attest
23 to the fact that the work was piled up for me by the time I got there. She couldn't have done a very
24 good job, to leave all the messages in such a messy state. It took me a few days just to sort everything
25 out and answer all the e-mail.

---

*   The transcript of Susan Robinson's deposition was excerpted so that only her answers are reprinted here. Assume
that this is a true and accurate rendering of those answers.

1   This deposition was taken in the office of plaintiff's counsel on July 27, YR -1. This deposition was
2   given under oath and was read and signed by the deponent.

Certified by:

Roger Powell
_____

Roger Powell
Certified Shorthand Reporter
(CSR)

OFFICE FLOOR PLAN

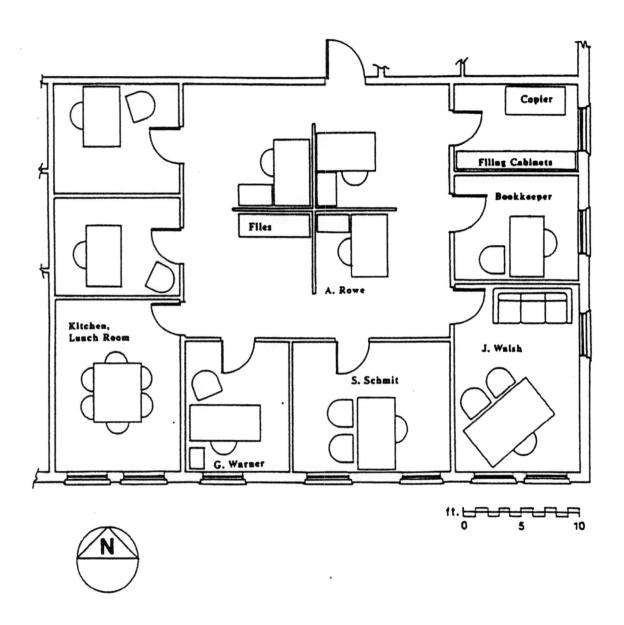

BENJAMIN J. COHEN

Attorney at Law
1341 Haven Court
Nita City, Nita 99990
(721) 555-0479

July 7, YR -1

Henry Glenn, Esq.
Glenn & O'Malley
100 Zee Street, Suite 801
Nita City, Nita 99990

RE: Alice Rowe v. Pacific Quad, Inc.

Dear Mr. Glenn:

In response to your Request to Produce Documents dated June 9, YR -1, I am enclosing two documents. One is a document entitled "COMPLAINT FORM," and the other is a document entitled "DECISION." Although I am certainly not willing to stipulate to the admissibility of the two documents, I am willing to stipulate that they are true and accurate copies of authentic business records of Nita State University.

Sincerely,

Benjamin J. Cohen

BJC:ak
Encls.

NITA STATE UNIVERSITY
STUDENT GRIEVANCE BOARD
COMPLAINT FORM

Please answer all of the following questions. Please type or print legibly in ink.

1. Name:

Alice Rowe

2. Local Address & Telephone:

1040 Redwood Lane, Nita City, Nita 99990   (721) 555-1047

3. Permanent Address & Telephone:

Same as #2

4. Against whom is this grievance being filed *(please give full name & department)*:

James Melvyl, Associate Professor, Dept. of History

5. Please describe in detail the circumstances and events which led to your filing this complaint. Try to be precise about the dates of discrete events. Use the back of this form for additional information.

I am currently enrolled in Prof. Melvyl's class "American History Through Literature." It is a small seminar; there are only about thirteen students. I began to notice at the beginning of the semester that Prof. Melvyl likes to stare at me intensely. He also makes sexual jokes
(over)

6. Please identify any persons who witnessed the events described above, who you believe would corroborate the allegations you have made here. Continue on the back of the form if necessary.

I am certain that all of the students in Prof. Melvyl's class will verify what I have said concerning Prof. Melvyl's conduct in the classroom. There are no witnesses, however,
(over)

SIGNATURE Alice Rowe   DATE 10-27-YR-5

GRIEVANCE BOARD COMPLAINT FORM ATTACHMENT

#5 (cont)

in class, mostly puns, and he always looks in my direction when doing so. I am certain that I am not mistaken about his behavior. It is so obvious that all of the students know what is going on.

I have been trying to ignore Prof. Melvyl's treatment of me, which I found offensive, humiliating, and degrading, but it has become impossible to do so any longer. Three weeks ago I was in his office discussing my paper for the course and he asked me to go out with him. Of course I said no. Later, when I confronted him, he denied the entire incident.

#6 (cont)

to Prof. Melvyl's attempt to proposition me in his office. I did relate this experience to Anna Mills, a counselor at the Women's Center, soon after it happened. I'm certain that she will corroborate how upset it made me.

NITA STATE UNIVERSITY
STUDENT GRIEVANCE BOARD DECISION

Complaining student: Alice Rowe

Complaint against: James Melvyl, Associate Professor
                                        Department of History

Nature of complaint: Sexual Harassment

Date of complaint: October 27, YR -5

Having investigated the complaint made by Ms. Rowe against
Professor Melvyl, including interviews of both parties and other
witnesses, it is the decision of the board that Ms. Rowe's
complaint is not supported by sufficient evidence to justify
further proceedings.

However, in view of the obvious strains that this complaint
has put on the teacher/student relationship between Professor
Melvyl and Ms. Rowe, it is the recommendation of this board
that Ms. Rowe should be permitted, if she chooses, to withdraw
from Professor Melvyl's course, and that Ms. Rowe's petition to
withdraw from the course should be treated as if it had been filed
before the November 1 deadline if she files it within 10 days of
this decision.

The complaint is DISMISSED.

November 15, YR -5

Alice Rowe

1040 Redwood Lane Nita City, Nita
(721) 555-1047

WORK EXPERICENCE

*   Leviathan Computers, 2600 Industrial Way, Nita City, Nita.
    Program Assistant
    January–August, YR -3.

*   Starbuck Software, 5301 Wharf Boulevard, Nita City, Nita.
    Administrative Assistant
    January–August, YR -4.

*   Nita Marine Insurance Company, 100 Ring Road, Nita City, Nita.
    Administrative Assistant
    September, YR -6–July, YR -5.

*   GAM Software, 53 53rd Street, Nita City, Nita.
    Administrative Assistant
    January–August, YR -6.

SKILLS

*   Proficient in Microsoft Office applications, MacIntosh applications, Adobe Acrobat PDF
    and Photoshop, graphic web design, LINXUS, DOS.

EDUCATION

*   Nita State University, Nita City, Nita. Completed 105 of 120 units required for B.S. in
    Computer Science. Grade point average 3.5

*   Central High School, Nita City, Nita. Diploma awarded, YR -10. National Honor Society.

PACIFIC QUAD, INC.
A NEW WAVE IN COMPUTERS

24 Beach Avenue Nita City, Nita 99998 (721) 555-5530

APPLICATION FOR EMPLOYMENT

1. Name: Alice Rowe

2. Address and Telephone: 1040 Redwood Lane, Nita City, Nita 99990 (721)555-1047

3. Sex: ( ) M (✓) F   4. Age: YR-26

5. Marital Status: Single (✓)   Married ( )   Divorced ( )   Separated ( )

6. Position sought: Secretary

7. Salary desired: Negotiable

8. Relevant educational and career experience: I have completed 105 out of 120 credits necessary for a B.S. in Computer Science at Nita State University. I graduated from Central High School, Nita City, in YR-10. (over)

9. How did you learn of the job opening? A friend of mine saw your advertisement

10. Have you ever been convicted for a criminal offense other than a traffic violation?
Yes ( ) No (✓) If yes, please explain: _____

_____

11. Are you under the care of a physician? Yes ( ) No (✓) A psychotherapist? Yes ( ) No ( )
If so, please explain: _____

_____

Please use the remaining space (and the reverse of this form, if necessary) to tell us anything else that you feel is relevant to your application for employment with Pacific Quad, Inc., or to further explain any answers given above.

I would like a career in the computer field and I feel that experience at Pacific Quad would be a good step towards that goal.

I hereby certify that all statements on this application are true and complete to the best of my knowledge and belief. If employed, I understand that any falsification of the above record may be considered cause of termination.

Date **2-2-yr-2**   Signature **Alice Roux**

#8(cont.)

I have been employed as a secretary by various local firms (mostly computer firms) over the last five years. Please refer to my resumé for further details.

PACIFIC QUAD, INC.
A NEW WAVE IN TECHNOLOGY
24 Beach Avenue Nita City, Nita 99998 (721) 555-5530

LIST OF PERMANENT EMPLOYEES
DURING THE PERIOD OF
FEBRUARY 1, YR -3 THROUGH MARCH 31, YR -2*

John Walsh (President)
24 Beach Avenue Nita City, Nita

Carolyn Kirk (Administrative Assistant)
1618 Pierre Way Nita City, Nita

Stanley Schmit (Operations Mgr.)
24 Beach Avenue Nita City, Nita

Liz Morrisey (Administrative Assistant)
1846 Typee Drive Nita City, Nita

Susan Robinson (Administrative Assistant)
24 Beach Avenue Nita City, Nita

Jason Novak (Director)
24 Beach Avenue Nita City, Nita

Sam Frigate (Shipping Clerk)
24 Beach Avenue Nita City, Nita

Opal Jennings (Administrative Assistant)
4066 Billybudd Road Nita City, Nita

Joey Lynch (Bookkeeper)
24 Beach Avenue Nita City, Nita

Alice Rowe (Administrative Assistant)
1040 Redwood Lane Nita City, Nita

Joyce Radville (Administrative Assistant)
24 Beach Avenue Nita City, Nita

Melinda Berger (Administrative Assistant)
789 "C" Street Nita City, Nita

Wilbur Matthews (Director)
24 Beach Avenue Nita City, Nita

Margaret Wilson (Administrative Assistant)
1452 Atlantic Boulevard Nita City, Nita

Robert Callahan (Sales Rep.)
24 Beach Avenue Nita City, Nita

Gloria Warner (Sales Rep.)
925 Ocean Way Nita City, Nita

Chris Kolbus (Administrative Assistant)
24 Beach Avenue Nita City, Nita

George McDermott (Sales Rep.)
24 Beach Avenue Nita City, Nita

Cindy Leonard (Administrative Assistant)
619 Benito Cerino Road Nita City, Nita

Richard Favorite (Sales Rep.)
24 Beach Avenue Nita City, Nita

This list includes both present and former employees with their business addresses as of October 1, YR -1. This document was produced by Pacific Quad, Inc., on October 16, YR - 1, in response to a written interrogatory submitted by the plaintiff's attorney, Benjamin Cohen.

PACIFIC QUAD, INC.
A NEW WAVE IN TECHNOLOGY

24 Beach Avenue Nita City, Nita 99998 (721) 555-5530

February 16, YR -2

Alice Rowe
1040 Redwood Lane
Nita City, Nita

Dear Ms. Rowe:

I am sorry that you will not be able to continue as a secretary with us. Even though you did not work a full day on Friday, February 11th, we have decided to pay you for the full week's work. We think that this is only fair, under all of the circumstances. Accordingly, please find enclosed a check for $569.77. Best wishes in your future employment.

Sincerely,

John Walsh

John Walsh
President

JW:oj
Encl: salary check for $569.77

NOTE

Pages 63 through 85 were supplied to the parties by the Nita Department of Fair Employment and Housing, pursuant to the Nita Public Records Act. The records are true and correct copies of the actual government files, and they shall be considered authentic. See required stipulation number 3 at pages 3–4.

DEPARTMENT OF FAIR EMPLOYMENT AND HOUSING

PRE-COMPLAINT QUESTIONNAIRE/EMPLOYMENT

The information requested on this form will help us to help you. There is no guarantee that the information submitted will constitute a basis for filing a formal complaint. If you need assistance in preparing this form, please ask the receptionist. When completed, give the form to the receptionist.

FOR OFFICIAL USE ONLY

Name of Interviewer: <u>Annie Cunningham</u>

Date of Interview: <u>March 23, YR -2</u>

PLEASE PRINT

Name: <u>Alice</u> <u>Rowe</u>
First   Middle   Last

Address: <u>1040 Redwood Lane</u>
Street   Apt. #

City: <u>Nita City</u>   County: <u>Nita</u>   Zip: <u>99990</u>

Telephone Number: Work ( )   Ext.

      Home <u>(721) 555-1047</u>

I prefer to be contacted by phone at work _____ at home __X__ days _____

Name: <u>Samuel C. Rowe</u>   Telephone: <u>(721) 555-1047</u>
(Person to contact if you cannot be reached)

I wish to complain against: (Name of employer, city, county, agency, etc.)

Name of Employer: <u>Pacific Quad, Inc.</u>

Street Address: <u>24 Beach Avenue</u>

City: <u>Nita City</u>   County: <u>Nita</u>   Zip: <u>99998</u>

Telephone Number: <u>(721) 555-5530</u>   Number of Employees: <u>12</u>

Others: _____

Street Address: _____

City: _____ County: _____ Zip: _____

1. I was discriminated against because of my (check only those which apply):

    ____Race   ____Color   ____National Origin/Ancestry
    _X_ Sex   ____Age (over 40)   ____Marital Status
    ____Medical Condition   ____Physical Handicap   ____Religion

2. How do you feel you were discriminated against?

    _X_ Termination   ____Denied Employment _X_ Harassment
    _X_ Differential Treatment   ____Denied Promotion   ____Other*(Please Specify)*

3. What reasons were given by the employer for the action taken against you?

    None given.

4. Date of alleged discrimination: February 7-11, YR -2

5. What remedy are you seeking through DFEH?

Stop the harassment, damages for my trauma, backpay until I can go back to work, and pay my medical bills.

6. Employment date:
    A. Date Hired: 2/3/YR -2
       Job Title: Administrative Assistant
    B. Date of Termination: 2/11/YR -2
       Job title at time of discrimination: Administrative Assistant
    C. Salary of position in question: $3,500/mo.
    D. Name of immediate supervisor: Stanley Schmit
    E. Is there a union? No   If so, name the union and local # _____

    F. Have you filed a union grievance? No   If so, name the union and local # _____

    G. Have you attempted to resolve your problem by discussing the matter with a representative of management? Yes

       If so, name the parties contacted: I talked to both Mr. Schmit and John Walsh.

H. If terminated, have you since been employed? Yes _____ No __X_____
    Name of company: _____ Date of hire: _____
    Job Title: _____ Salary: _____

7. What information do you have to indicate that you were treated differently because of discrimination?

I was hired as an administrative assistant but when I

reported to work, I was continually harassed by my

supervisor Mr. Schmit. By the end of the week, I couldn't

put up with him anymore. Then he propositioned me and so I

told him that I didn't have to tolerate such treatment.

When I complained, they only told me to leave so I did.

8. List the names, job titles and telephone numbers (if possible) of witnesses you feel could provide evidence in your support.

Name	Title	Telephone Numbers Home	Work
Anna Mills	Counselor		(721)555-0038

9. Did you file a complaint with EEOC before coming to this agency? Yes _____ No __X____

10. Complaints other than marital status, medical condition and physical handicap filed with DFEH are often simultaneously filed with the Equal Employment Opportunity Commission of the federal government. (Employer must have sixteen or more employees) and alleged act must have occurred within three hundred days of filing.) In no way does this delay the complaint being processed by this agency. If your complaint is accessed by DFEH, do you wish a copy forwarded to EEOC?
Yes __X____ No _____

11. Have you filed with any other group or agency? Yes _____ No __X_____
If so, name, address, and telephone numbers are requested.

12. Do you have an attorney? Yes _____ No __X_____
    If so, please provide name, address, and telephone number.

    _____

    _____

    _____

PERSONAL DATA

13. For research purposes, please provide us with the following information:

    ETHNIC GROUP:
    Black _____Hispanic_____Asian _____ Filipino_____Anglo _X_____

    Native American_____Other Minority *(Please Specify)*_____

    SEX: Female ___X_____ Male _____

    AGE: __26_____

14. I learned about the Department of Fair Employment and Housing from:

    Newspaper_____Radio_____TV_____Bus/BART Ad_____Poster__X_____

    Friend Prior Contact with DFEH_____Other Government Agency_____

    Community Organizations *(Please Specify)*_____

    Other *(Please Specify)*_____

(Do Not Write in This Area)

INTERVIEWER'S NOTES

Ms. Rowe alleges sexual harassment during her one week of work at Pacific Quad, Inc. Ms. Rowe alleges that her immediate supervisor, Stanley Schmit, propositioned her on Friday, February 11. When Ms. Rowe complained about the harassment and demanded that Mr. Schmit stop such behavior, Mr. Schmit refused and Ms. Rowe left the office. She believes that she was forced to leave. Ms. Rowe does not remember the words of the proposition but remembers that Mr. Schmit had a big smile on his face and a leering look in his eyes.

DEPARTMENT OF FAIR EMPLOYMENT AND HOUSING

CASE DIARY
Alice Rowe
#FEP 03-02-A0-000se

Complainant _Alice Rowe_   Case _____

Message Telephone (__)_____   EEOC/HUD#_____

Filing Date _March 23, YR -2_____   Service Date _____

Respondent _Pacific Quad, Inc._____   Co-Respondent _____

Respondent Contact Person: Co-Respondent Contact Person:

Name _John Walsh_____   Name _____

Title _President_____   Title _____

Address _24 Beach Avenue, Nita City_   Address _____

Telephone _(721) 555-5530_____   Telephone (__)_____

Respondent's formal representative to receive closure letter:

Name_____   Title _____

Address _____

Complainant's Change of Address #1:   Complainant's Change of Address #2:

Date notified_____   Date notified _____

Address_____   Address _____

Telephone (__)_____   Telephone (__)_____

ACTIVITY CODES:

IN INVESTIGATION—Begins when complaint is filed and includes activities with sole purpose of obtaining information on case for closure or accusation, including interrogatories and subpoenas.

S/C SETTLEMENT/CONCILIATION—Includes activities involved in reaching a settlement prior to submittal for accusation.

RW REPORT WRITING—Includes progress memos and closing reports.

PH PUBLIC HEARING—Activities performed after a case has been referred to legal for accusation.

TIME—To be entered in increments of no less than 15 minutes.

Date & Initials	Case Activity	Activity Time Code	Hr Min
YR -2 3/23	complaint filed served		
4/6	rec'd response to service letter from Walsh		
4/20	called Walsh RE: anti-harassment policy; explained DFEH procedures		
4/22	called complainant to update on case		
4/26	called Walsh RE: respondent's account of facts		
5/3	complainant came into office to sign Release forms, denies Walsh's account of facts		
5/5	called Anna Mills complainant's counselor; will help in any way she can		
5/17	called Walsh RE: settlement possibilities(talked to Robinson— doesn't remember Walsh ever asking her to correct any mistakes in first letter to DFEH)		
6/21	rec'd Walsh letter and Robinson affidavit		
8/30	rec'd call from Gloria Warner		
9/10	issued right-to-sue letter to complainant		
9/17	rec'd call from B. Cohen. Claims he will soon be filing private action for complainant. I told him that when he did I will close case.		
11/23	closed case—complainant elected court action.		

TOTAL TIME

District Office Time (record in total hours and/or minutes)   **Legal Time**   **TOTAL**

IN= _____   S/C= _____   RW= _____   PH= _____   _____   _____

CHARGE OF DISCRIMINATION

This form is affected by the Privacy Act of 1974; see Privacy Act Statement on reverse before completing this form.

ENTER CHARGE NUMBER __FEPA 03-02 AO 000se__ EEOC __N/A__

__Nita Department of Fair Employment and Housing__ and EEOC
(State or local Agency, if any)

Name (Indicate Mr., Ms., or Mrs.)	Home Telephone No.
Ms. Alice Rowe	(721) 555-1047

Address	City	State	County
1040 Redwood Lane	Nita	City Nita	Nita

NAMED IS THE EMPLOYER, LABOR ORGANIZATION, EMPLOYMENT AGENCY, APPRENTICESHIP COMMITTEE, STATE OR LOCAL GOVERNMENT AGENCY WHO DISCRIMINATED AGAINST ME (If more than one list below.)

Name	No. of Employees/Members	Telephone (Area Code)
Pacific Quad, Inc.	12	(721) 555-5530

Address	City	State	County
24 Beach Avenue	Nita	City Nita	Nita

Name	No. of Employees/Members	Telephone (Area Code)

Address	City	State	County

Cause of discrimination based on: *(Check appropriate boxes)*

□Race □Color ☒Sex □Religion □National Origin □Age

□Retaliation □Other *(Specify)* _____

Date most recent or continuing discrimination took place (mo.,day,year)

__Feb. 12, YR -2__

The particulars are (if additional space is needed, attach extra sheets)

1. On Thursday, February 3, YR -2, I applied for and was hired for the position of administrative assistant at Pacific Quad, Inc. I was interviewed by the operations manager, Stanley Schmit.

2. When I reported to work the next Monday, February 7, YR -2, Mr. Schmit, my immediate supervisor, began sexually harassing me. This harassment continued all week long. The harassment included the following:

    A.   Mr. Schmit propositioned me and used sexual innuendoes.

    B.   Mr. Schmit was watching me very closely. I felt that his eyes were constantly on my body.

3. As a woman, I refuse to be subjected to such abuse and demanded that Mr. Schmit stop his harassment. When he refused to do so, I spoke with Mr. Schmit's supervisor, the president of the company, Mr. John Walsh. Mr. Walsh refused to discipline Mr. Schmit and told me to leave.

☒ I also want this charge filed with the EEOC. I will advise the agencies if I change my address or telephone number and I will cooperate fully with them in the processing of my charge in accordance with their procedures.

I declare under penalty of perjury that the foregoing is true and correct.

I swear or affirm that I have read the above charge and that it is true to the best of my knowledge, information and belief.

SIGNATURE OF COMPLAINANT

alice Rowe

NOTARY (when necessary to meet state and local requirements)

SUBSCRIBED AND SWORN TO BEFORE ME THIS DATE

_____

My Commission Expires:

_____

PACIFIC QUAD, INC.
A NEW WAVE IN TECHNOLOGY
24 Beach Avenue Nita City, Nita 99998 (721) 555-5530

April 1, YR -2

Ms. Annie Cunningham
Department of Fair Employment & Housing
30 Van Ness Avenue
Nita City, Nita 99990

Dear Ms. Cunningham:

I have received the discrimination complaint from your office, but I frankly do not understand what the problem is. Our records do show that Alice Rowe worked for us for one week in February, but she quit without any explanation, not because of any sexual harassment. I have spoken to my operations manager, Stanley Schmit, about Ms. Rowe, and he has assured me that discrimination had nothing to do with Ms. Rowe's abrupt departure. Stan never propositioned Ms. Rowe or sexually harassed her.

I personally never knew that Ms. Rowe had any complaints until I talked to Stan on Friday afternoon, February 12th. Stan told me that he didn't know why Ms. Rowe left and that he had just assumed that she had decided not to work here after all—secretaries are often like that. You can see that we are very surprised by this complaint.

Frankly, I am very disturbed by this discrimination charge because we have a very strong anti-harassment policy here at Pacific Quad. This company was started by myself and two other friends from BMI in August YR -4. I am the principal shareholder and am responsible for the general operations of the company. Thus, you can see that I take this matter personally. I am very disturbed that someone with an overactive imagination would accuse us of such behavior. We are still a very small company of twelve employees, and we like to think of ourselves as a family. This charge has disrupted our work environment and has already taken up a lot of precious time and energy. I would like to cooperate with you in any way I can to resolve this unfortunate misunderstanding. Please feel free to contact me directly if you have any further questions.

Sincerely,

John Walsh
President

JW:sr

INVESTIGATOR'S NOTES
Annie Cunningham

DATE: April 20, YR -2
CASE: Rowe/Pacific Quad, Inc.
           FEP 03-02 A0-000se

called John Walsh RE: his response letter of April 1
explained case still open/active and am proceeding with
investigation

asked whether his "anti-harassment policy" was in writing; he
replied that it was not but that it had often been discussed
informally; that the company was "very sensitive to the needs of
modern women"

asked whether Pacific Quad had any documentary evidence to
support their denial of discrimination; Walsh responded that
he didn't remember the details himself and that since Pacific
Quad was a small and new company, didn't really have any past
resignations or terminations; expressed concern about the privacy
of employee records

tried to explain the importance of the submission of some
documentary evidence, especially regarding the reason why
complainant resigned—Walsh was confused about DFEH authority
to investigate/prosecute, explained investigatory/conciliation
powers and accusation/hearing process

Walsh expressed a desire to avoid any litigation/publicity;
didn't think the matter was that serious but wanted to cooperate;
said that he would try to gather some documentary evidence and
will send to DFEH as soon as possible

INVESTIGATOR'S NOTES
Annie Cunningham

DATE: April 22, YR -2
CASE: Rowe/Pacific Quad, Inc.
           FEP 03-02 A0-000se

called complainant Alice Rowe to give her an update on the case
informed her of Walsh's response of April 1 and telephone
conversation with Walsh on April 20

Rowe strongly denies that she quit without giving Schmit or Walsh
any reason; says she plainly told Schmit after he propositioned
her on Friday, "I don't have to put up with this—I'm not going to
play your games."

Rowe also strongly denies that Walsh didn't know about her
complaint of sexual harassment; says she went to Walsh's office
after Schmit propositioned her on Friday, February 11th; however,
Walsh told her, "I can't be bothered—if you're not happy with the
job, you can leave." —Rowe left

Rowe denies that there was any anti-harassment policy—she never
saw any in writing and never heard of one

Rowe has been seeing a counselor to help her overcome the trauma
—she has been told to stay off work for now

INVESTIGATOR'S NOTES
Annie Cunningham

DATE: April 26, YR -2
CASE: Rowe/Pacific Quad, Inc.
           FEP 03-02 A0-000se

called Walsh RE: phone conversation with complainant on April 22

Walsh admits that he talked to Rowe on Friday, February 11 and says that he had told his secretary Susan to change the sentence in the letter about not knowing anything about Rowe's resignation; says things have been very busy around the office and he hasn't been concentrating on the complaint.

Walsh now remembers that Rowe came into his office at around noon on Friday, February 11, the last day that Rowe worked; Walsh says that Rowe was very upset—her eyes were very wet and red, and it looked as if she had been crying

Walsh couldn't quite understand everything Rowe said—began mumbling and sobbing at the same time—maybe something about her not being able to get along with men and that "this always happens to me"; Walsh says that he was pretty confused and didn't know what she was talking about but that eventually she calmed down

Walsh asked if there was anything he could do and suggested that she could leave for a break—he thought that maybe the fresh air would help her and it was time for her lunch break anyway; Walsh strongly denies saying that he couldn't be bothered or suggesting that she quit

Walsh says that Rowe never came back—when he didn't see her at her desk later that afternoon, Walsh asked Schmit about her and Schmit said that she had told him that she was quitting, without giving any reason; Schmit thought that maybe she had some personal problems and just couldn't handle the job because she had been agitated all week long

Walsh again denies that there was any harassment

INVESTIGATOR'S NOTES
Annie Cunningham

```
DATE:      May 3, YR -2
CASE:      Rowe/Pacific Quad, Inc.
           FEP 03-02 A0-000se
```

Complainant came in to sign release forms (for work related and medical records)

discussed with Complainant the phone conversation with Walsh on April 26; Complainant denies that she was hysterical or incomprehensible—states that if she was upset, it was because of the entire week of harassment and the proposition by Schmit

Asked Complainant for more details about the harassment; Schmit constantly commented on how she looked—how he liked a certain dress or outfit; it was his tone of voice and the look in his eyes that made her feel that he was making sexual innuendoes

Once, Schmit said something about her work but there were sexual innuendoes about her doing a "good job"

Schmit would often use sexually explicit language in instructions or just in casual conversations with the Complainant, in reference to items that the company developed or just in his expressions; Rowe found his language vulgar and offensive

Complainant also detailed the proposition on Friday; Schmit said something about asking her to go out to dinner or for drinks—she can't remember the exact words but does remember that Schmit was leering and winking; when she refused and asked why, Schmit said, "It's business."

Complainant asked what kind of business required that they go out for dinner over the weekend; Schmit said, "We'll see what comes up"—Complainant interpreted this as a sexual proposition. Complainant admits that she had been crying before going in to see Walsh; she did not go directly from her desk to Walsh's office but stopped at the bathroom first

Complainant vehemently denies that Walsh did not understand her; states that she made it quite clear that she was leaving because of Schmit's harassment

continued...

INVESTIGATOR'S NOTES
May 3, YR -2
Continued...

Complainant states that she felt forced to leave the job; that after talking to Walsh, she was so disgusted and frustrated that she simply picked up her purse and told Schmit, "I'm quitting" and then left

Asked Complainant for more details about Schmit's language, expressions, propositions. She said this was all she could recall—became upset at me and accused me of not believing her

INVESTIGATOR'S NOTES
Annie Cunningham

DATE: May 17, YR -2
CASE: Rowe v. Pacific Quad, Inc.
            FEP 03-02 A0-OOOse

called Walsh RE: settlement possibilities, explained to Walsh
that the key to settlement was:

1) formal institution of an anti-harassment policy

2) back pay, out-of-pocket medical expenses, and some
compensatory damages for Complainant

Walsh rejected any monetary damages; said he would have Schmit
write a formal apology to Rowe and that he would sign it—but
that's all

Walsh stated that "maybe Stan did use some colorful language—so
what?" and that Schmit never intended to offend or embarrass
anyone

Walsh also continues to deny that any propositioning or
harassment took place—attributes Rowe's account to her overactive
imagination; that "just being friendly" is not harassment

told Walsh that DFEH would continue to gather evidence and
investigate but would also continue to be open to settlement
offers

INVESTIGATOR'S NOTES
Annie Cunningham

DATE: August 30, YR -2
CASE: Rowe/Pacific Quad, Inc.
           FEP 03-02 A0-OOOse

rec'd call from Gloria Warner RE: Rowe case

Warner is a sales representative at Pacific Quad

found out about complaint because Stanley Schmit came over to her desk and showed her a copy of it

Warner remembers a conversation between Schmit and John Walsh at around the same time Rowe was hired—Schmit told Walsh, "Hey, I've just hired a real babe as my secretary"—Warner is pretty sure that Schmit was referring to Rowe but cannot be positive—can't remember the exact dates involved

Warner looked up DFEH phone number in phone book because she thought the information might help—doesn't remember anything else about Rowe

Warner has not experienced any sexual advances at Pacific Quad but she has often felt that Stanley Schmit was "undressing" her with his eyes; does not know of any other cases or complaints of harassment at Pacific Quad

PACIFIC QUAD, INC.
A NEW WAVE IN TECHNOLOGY

24 Beach Avenue Nita City, Nita 99998 (721) 555-5530

June 17, YR -2

Ms. Annie Cunningham
Department of Fair Employment & Housing
30 Van Ness Avenue
Nita City, Nita 99990

Dear Ms. Cunningham:

Please find attached a statement from Ms. Susan Robinson regarding the Alice Rowe case. I do hope that we may resolve this matter soon. If I can be of further assistance, please do not hesitate to let me know. Thank you for your attention.

Sincerely,

John Walsh
President

JW:sr
Attachment

I, Susan Robinson, declare:

I am currently employed as a secretary at Pacific Quad, Inc. I have lived in Nita City all my life and have been employed as an administrative assistant in a variety of offices and businesses. During my years as an administrative assistant, I have worked for many executives and have had to work closely with many of them. I can attest to the good character of my current supervisor, Stanley Schmit. Mr. Schmit has always treated me with the greatest respect and courtesy. He has always acted in a highly professional manner and is a model of gentlemanly behavior. I am somewhat shocked to learn of this false accusation against Mr. Schmit. In all the years that I have known Mr. Schmit, I have never seen him conduct himself in any way that would even remotely suggest sexual harassment. I am sure Mr. Schmit will be vindicated in this matter.

Executed on June 17, YR -2, at Nita City, Nita.

I declare under penalty of perjury that the foregoing is true and correct.

Susan Robinson

NITA STATE UNIVERSITY

WOMEN'S CENTER
ANNA MILLS, L.C.S.W.

July 22, YR -2

Saul:

Thank you for agreeing to be on call for my clients while I will be away in New York. I did want to alert you about one of my patients, Alice Rowe, whom I have been seeing for about three years. Alice is a single, twenty-six-year-old woman who came to me for career counseling and relational difficulties.

Currently, Alice has one more year of college before graduation but has repeatedly dropped out of school to take part-time secretarial jobs because of a fear of success and lack of self-esteem. Through counseling we have traced much of Alice's self-defeating attitude to her parental relationship. Alice is an only child, with a hypercritical father and a passive mother. She grew up feeling inadequate, non-assertive, and withdrawn. In addition to her academic and career problems, she has had a continuing conflict with her own femininity.

Although counseling was often difficult, Alice had been making considerable progress and she had a genuine feeling of optimism about the future. She was feeling strong enough to go back to school full-time in September, YR -3, to finish her degree in computer science. There was marked improvement in her self-motivation and sense of independence.

However, in February of this year, Alice suffered a significant setback because of a reported incident of sexual harassment at a new job. She was seriously debilitated by the perceived harassment and has been unable to work ever since. She has suffered from insomnia and nightmares. Through increased and intensive counseling, she has made a partial recovery, to the point where she may be ready to go back to work soon. Since the possibility of another misunderstood encounter with a man is very real, I wanted to alert you to Alice's condition. I have discussed your availability with her, and she will be calling on you if she feels the need for counseling or discussion.

Thanks again. I hope all this won't be too much trouble for you.

Anna

Anna

DEPARTMENT OF FAIR EMPLOYMENT AND HOUSING
30 Van Ness Avenue   Nita City, Nita 99990

September 10, YR -2

Alice Rowe
1040 Redwood Lane
Nita City, Nita 99998

     re: FEP 03-02 A0-000se

Dear Ms. Rowe:

Your complaint of discrimination (identified above) is on file
with our office. According to the law, the Department must notify
you of your right to file a private lawsuit in a Nita Superior
Court on your own behalf. This letter is your notification of that
right.

No action is required by you unless you decide to file a private
lawsuit. If you choose to exercise this option you must:
    1) Notify the Department in writing of your intent; and
    2) Provide your own legal counsel; and
    3) File your case within one year from the date of this
    letter.

The Department will continue to process your complaint unless you
advise them otherwise. If you do not wish to file a civil suit
under Nita law, you need not respond to this letter.

Sincerely,

Mark Alber
District Administrator
cc: Henry Glenn

IN THE COURT OF APPEALS OF THE STATE OF NITA
FIRST DISTRICT
DIVISION 6

ALICE ROWE,   )
Appellant and Plaintiff,   )
)
v.   )   Civ. No. 0-09876543
)
PACIFIC QUAD, INC.,   )   OPINION
Respondent and Defendant,   )

Argued and Submitted April 1, YR -1
Decided April 25, YR -1

BEFORE: Duba, Presiding Justice, and
        Hamater and Pierson, Associate Justices

HAMATER, Justice.

This case comes to this court upon an appeal from a final judgment of dismissal in favor of the defendant in the Superior Court of the County of Darrow after granting the defendant's motion to dismiss for failure to state a claim and granting a motion to strike the prayers for compensatory and punitive damages. For the reasons set forth herein, we reverse.

I. FACTS.

Appellant Alice Rowe brought suit in the Superior Court of Darrow County alleging that respondent Pacific Quad, Inc., discriminated against her in violation of Nita Government Code section 12940. Rowe filed a complaint with the Department of Fair Employment and Housing on March 23, YR -2. After its investigation of the complaint, but before the Department had made a determination whether to prosecute, Rowe decided to withdraw her complaint and file a civil action. Pursuant to Nita Government Code section 12965, Rowe filed her action in the Superior Court, County of Darrow, on November 3, YR -2. On November 21, YR -2, defendant filed a motion to dismiss for failure to state a claim and moved to strike the prayers for compensatory and punitive damages. By an Order dated December 15, YR -2, the Superior Court, Nolan, J., sustained the motion to dismiss with leave to amend and granted the motion to strike. Rowe did not amend her complaint and a final judgment of dismissal was entered on January 15, YR -1. Rowe then brought this appeal.

In determining whether the motion to dismiss was properly sustained by the Superior Court, this Court must assume the facts alleged in the complaint to be true. *Tameny v. Atlantic Richfield Co.*, 27 Nita 3d 167 (1980); *Strauss v. A.L. Randall Co., Inc.*, 144 Nita App. 3d 514 (2d Dist. 1983).

Briefly summarized, Rowe alleges that she began employment at Pacific Quad in the position of administrative assistant on February 8, YR -2. She further alleges that beginning that day and throughout the week, her immediate supervisor, Operations Manager Stanley Schmit, subjected her to repeated verbal sexual abuse and on February 11, YR -2, made an unsolicited and unwanted sexual advance toward her. She also alleges that both Schmit and Pacific Quad President John Walsh conditioned her continued employment upon her consenting to Schmit's sexual demands. Finally, Rowe alleges that she was constructively terminated in retaliation for her refusal to consent to Schmit's sexual advances.

II. SEXUAL HARASSMENT VIOLATIVE OF THE FAIR EMPLOYMENT AND HOUSING ACT.

The facts alleged, if proven at trial, would require a legal finding of unlawful discrimination in the terms and conditions of employment under the Fair Employment and Housing Act (hereinafter "FEHA"). Nita Gov't Code § 12940(a); *see also* Nita Admin. Code, tit. 2, §§ 7287.6(b), 7291.1(f)(1).

There are no published decisions of the Nita Courts directly analyzing sexual harassment as a violation of the Nita FEHA. However, the Nita FEHA was modeled after the California FEHA and Title VII of the 1964 Civil Rights Act, which have spawned a number of precedents from the California and federal courts. These decisions provide a detailed analysis of sexual harassment under the California FEHA and Title VII, and provide us with helpful guidance in determining our own standard. Thus, the following analysis draws extensively on California law as well as federal law.

In *Lyle v. Warner Brothers*, 132 P.3d 211, 219 (Cal. 2006), the California Supreme Court held:

> With certain exceptions not implicated here, the FEHA makes it an unlawful employment practice for an employer, "because of the . . . sex . . . of any person, . . . to discriminate against the person in compensation or in terms, conditions, or privileges of employment." (§ 12940, subd. (a).) Likewise, it is an unlawful employment practice for an employer, "because of . . . sex, . . . to harass an employee." (§ 12940, subd. (j)(1).) Under the statutory scheme, "'harassment' because of sex" includes sexual harassment and gender harassment. (§ 12940, subd. (j)(4)(C).) These prohibitions represent a fundamental public policy decision regarding "the need to protect and safeguard the right and opportunity of all persons to seek and hold employment free from discrimination." (*Brown v. Superior Court* (1984) 37 Cal. 3d 477, 485, 208 Cal. Rptr. 724, 691 P.2d 272; see also *Mogilefsky v. Superior Court* (1993) 20 Cal. App. 4th 1409, 1414, 26 Cal. Rptr. 2d 116.)

That Court continued, citing its own earlier decisions: "'the prohibition against sexual harassment includes protection from a broad range of conduct, ranging from expressly or impliedly conditioning employment benefits on submission to or tolerance of unwelcome sexual advances, to the creation of a work environment that is hostile or abusive on the basis of sex.'" *Id.* at 219 (quoting *Miller v. Dep't of Corr.*, 115 P.3d 77 (Cal. 2005)).

The *Lyle* Court further held that under the California FEHA and

> Title VII, a hostile work environment sexual harassment claim requires a plaintiff employee to show she was subjected to sexual advances, conduct, or comments that were (1) unwelcome (see *Meritor, supra,* 477 U.S. at p. 68); (2) because of sex (*Oncale v. Sundowner Offshore Services, Inc.* (1998) 523 U.S. 75, 80-81, 118 S.Ct. 998, 140 L.Ed.2d 201 (*Oncale*)); and (3) sufficiently severe or

pervasive to alter the conditions of her employment and create an abusive work environment (*id.* at p. 81; *Meritor, supra,* 477 U.S. at p. 67). In addition, she must establish the offending conduct was imputable to her employer. (*Meritor, supra,* 477 U.S. at pp. 69-73) California courts have adopted the same standard for hostile work environment sexual harassment claims under the FEHA. (See, e.g., *Fisher v. San Pedro Peninsula Hospital* (1989) 214 Cal. App. 3d 590, 608, 262 Cal. Rptr. 842.)

Lyle, 132 P.3d at 220.

A. Sexual Harassment.

Sexual harassment is defined by the Nita Code as "verbal, physical, and visual harassment, and unwanted sexual advances." Nita Admin. Code, tit. 2, § 7291.1(f)(1), 7287.6(b). Verbal harassment, as defined by the Nita Code, includes "epithets, derogatory comments, or slurs." Nita Admin. Code, tit. 2, § 7287(b)(1).

Pacific Quad asserts that Rowe's claims cannot meet this definition. The key phrase in the Nita FEHA for determining sexual harassment is that there must be "unwanted sexual conduct." Each word of this phrase represents a distinct test. First, a plaintiff must prove that the alleged *conduct* actually occurred. Second, the plaintiff must prove, by a subjective standard, that the conduct was *unwanted.* Third, the trier of fact must determine whether a reasonable person would interpret the words or actions of the defendant, in light of all the surrounding circumstances, to be sexual.

We find that the facts alleged, if true, meet this definition of sexual harassment.

B. Adversely Affected Employment Benefit.

If sexual harassment did occur, the next issue is whether the sexual harassment affects the complainant adversely by depriving her of an employment benefit. *See* Nita Admin. Code, tit. 2, § 7286.5(f). There are three employment benefits that may be adversely affected.

1. Termination.

An employer terminates an employee when continued employment is conditioned upon accession to sexual demands. Nita Admin. Code, tit. 2, § 7287.6(b)(1)(D). The condition can be express or implied. Here, plaintiff alleges that such a condition was implied when John Walsh told her to leave if she was not happy with the job. Thus, Alice Rowe states facts that would support a finding of termination, a clearly adverse action.

2. Constructive Termination.

Victims of sexual harassment may be forced to quit jobs they otherwise enjoy because they are no longer able to tolerate the offending behavior. Constructive termination occurs where the working conditions are so intolerable that the employee could not be reasonably expected to have remained at her job.

Here, complainant alleges that she was forced to resign because of Stanley Schmit's sexual harassment and the non-responsiveness of John Walsh to take any corrective action. This, too, if proven, constitutes an adverse action.

3. Hostile Work Environment.

Even when there are no conditions placed upon the employee that lead to a termination or constructive termination, the employer may still be liable for a violation of the FEHA if the sexual harassment created a hostile work environment. A discrimination-free workplace or a work environment free of sexual harassment is itself an employment benefit that may not be adversely affected by an employer.

As the California Supreme Court explained in *Miller v. Department of Corrections*, 115 P.3d 77, 87–88 (Cal. 2005):

> According to the Fair Employment and Housing Commission (FEHC), the agency charged with administering the FEHA, harassment on any basis prohibited by the FEHA includes (but is not limited to) *verbal harassment*, including "epithets, derogatory comments or slurs on a basis enumerated in the Act"; physical harassment, including "assault, impeding or blocking movement, or any physical interference with normal work or movement,

when directed at an individual on a basis enumerated in the Act"; and visual harassment, including "derogatory posters, cartoons, or drawings on a basis enumerated in the Act." (Cal. Code Regs., tit. 2, § 7287.6, subd. (b)(1)(A), (B) & (C).) The regulations also specify that "unwanted sexual advances which condition an employment benefit upon an exchange of sexual favors" constitute harassment. (*Id.*, § 7287.6, subd. (b)(1)(D).) In the specific context of sexual discrimination, prohibited harassment may include "verbal, physical, and visual harassment, as well as unwanted sexual advances." (*Id.*, § 7291.1 subd. (f)(1).)

Past California decisions have established that the prohibition against sexual harassment includes protection from a broad range of conduct, ranging from expressly or impliedly conditioning employment benefits on submission to or tolerance of unwelcome sexual advances, to the creation of a work environment that is hostile or abusive on the basis of sex. (*Fisher v. San Pedro Peninsula Hospital* (1989) 214 Cal. App. 3d 590, 607-608, 262 Cal. Rptr. 842; see also *Mogilefsky v. Superior Court* (1993) 20 Cal. App. 4th 1409, 1414-1415, 26 Cal. Rptr. 2d 116.). . . . We have agreed with the United States Supreme Court that, to prevail, an employee claiming harassment based upon a hostile work environment must demonstrate that the conduct complained of was severe enough or sufficiently pervasive to alter the conditions of employment and create a work environment that qualifies as hostile or abusive to employees because of their sex. (See *Aguilar v. Avis Rent A Car System, Inc., supra,* 21 Cal. 4th at p. 130, 87 Cal. Rptr. 2d 132, 980 P.2d 846, relying upon *Harris v. Forklift Systems, Inc.* (1993) 510 U.S. 17, 21, 114 S.Ct. 367, 126 L.Ed.2d 295.) The working environment must be evaluated in light of the totality of the circumstances: "[W]hether an environment is 'hostile' or 'abusive' can be determined only by looking at all the circumstances. These may include the frequency of the discriminatory conduct; its severity; whether it is physically threatening or humiliating, or a mere offensive utterance; and whether it unreasonably interferes with an employee's work performance." (*Harris v. Forklift Systems, Inc.*, *supra*, 510 U.S. at p. 23, 114 S.Ct. 367.)

The appellant alleges that Schmit subjected her to an entire week of verbal sexual harassment and then made an unsolicited and unwanted sexual advance toward her. Such facts are sufficient to support a finding that plaintiff was subjected to a hostile work environment, which constitutes an adverse action.

C. Employer Liability.

The last element of a cause of action for sexual harassment under the FEHA is that the employer be liable for the sexual harassment. In this regard, there is a difference between Nita law, which follows California law, and federal law under Title VII.

Under California law, which Nita has adopted, an employer is strictly liable under the FEHA for sexual harassment by a supervisor. *See State Department of Health Services v. Superior Court*, 79 P.3d 556 (Cal. 2003). But the avoidable consequences doctrine applies to damage claims under the FEHA, and under that doctrine a plaintiff's recoverable damages do not include those damages that the plaintiff could have avoided with reasonable effort and without undue risk, expense, or humiliation. *Id.*

As the court explained,

> In this particular context, the defense has three elements: (1) the employer took reasonable steps to prevent and correct workplace sexual harassment; (2) the employee unreasonably failed to use the preventive and corrective measures that the employer provided; and (3) reasonable use of the employer's procedures would have prevented at least some of the harm that the employee suffered.

> This defense will allow the employer to escape liability for those damages, and only those damages, that the employee more likely than not could have prevented with reasonable effort and without undue risk, expense, or humiliation, by taking advantage of the employer's internal complaint procedures appropriately designed to prevent and eliminate sexual harassment.

Id. at 565.

By contrast, under Title VII, in cases involving sexual harassment not involving a "tangible employment action," such as demotion or termination, an employer may establish a partial or complete defense by proving: "(a) that the employer exercised reasonable care to prevent and correct promptly any sexually harassing behavior, and (b) that the plaintiff employee unreasonably failed to take advantage of any preventive or corrective opportunities provided by the employer or to avoid harm otherwise." *Burlington Industries, Inc. v. Ellerth*, 524 U.S. 742, 765 (1998); *Faragher v. City of Boca Raton*, 524 U.S. 775, 807 (1998).

Accordingly, we reverse the judgment of dismissal in favor of the defendant Pacific Quad, Inc., and remand the case with instructions to the trial court to vacate its order sustaining the motion to dismiss and enter an order denying it. We now turn to the question of damages raised by the motion to strike. We also reverse the trial court's decision on this motion, and direct the reinstatement of the prayers for compensatory and punitive damages.

III. RELIEF UNDER THE FAIR EMPLOYMENT AND HOUSING ACT FOR UNLAWFUL SEXUAL HARASSMENT.

The respondent Pacific Quad, Inc., has objected to the plaintiff's request for compensatory and punitive damages. The Nita Supreme Court has held, however, that compensatory and punitive damages are available to remedy violations of the FEHA. *Commodore Homes Systems, Inc. v. Superior Court*, 32 Nita 3d 211 (1982). Respondent asserts that *Commodore* is distinguishable because it involved race discrimination, which is entitled to greater legal protection. The case cannot be so narrowly read.

Compensatory damages are properly available to compensate the victim of sexual harassment for the intangible, but nonetheless very real, injury suffered in the form of fear, emotional distress, shame, and humiliation.

Exemplary or punitive damages are also available under Nita law where the employer's actions in violation of the FEHA are sufficiently oppressive, fraudulent, or malicious. Nita Civil Code § 3294; *Commodore Homes Systems, Inc. v. Superior Court, supra*. Nita Civil Code section 3294 specifically authorizes punitive damages where there is oppression, fraud, or malice. Malice exists where there is conduct that is intended to vex, injure, harass, or annoy, or that is taken in conscious disregard of the rights or safety of others. Oppression exists where a person is subjected to cruel and unjust hardship in conscious disregard of that person's rights. Nita Civil Code § 3294(c); *Kreiger v. Pacific Gas and Electric Co.*, 119 Nita App. 3d 137, 148 (3d Dist. 1981).

A corporate employer is liable for punitive damages for the acts of oppression, fraud, or malice of an officer, director, or managing agent of the corporation. A corporate employer may also be held liable for punitive damages for the acts of oppression, fraud, or malice of any other employee of the corporation if an officer, director, or managing agent of the corporation ratifies those actions. Nita Civil Code § 3294(b); *Agarwal v. Johnson*, 25 Nita 3d 932, 951 (1979); *Egan v. Mutual of Omaha Insurance Co.*, 24 Nita 3d 809, 822 (1979); *see also DFEH v. Donald Schriver, Inc.*, *supra.*, at 19.

A managing agent is a person who is vested with sufficient authority that he or she is helping to run the company. Some examples of a managing agent's functions are hiring and firing, disciplining employees, and purchasing important items for company use.

A corporation may also be held liable for conduct of other employees if it ratifies such conduct. Ratification may be established by circumstantial or direct evidence demonstrating adoption or approval of the employee's actions by the corporate agent. *Hale v. Farmer's Insurance Exchange*, 42 Nita App. 3d 681, 692 (4th Dist. 1974). Such ratification may be inferred from the fact that the employer, after being informed of the employee's actions, does not fully investigate and fails to repudiate the employee's conduct by redressing the harm done and punishing or discharging the offending employee. *Sandoval v. Southern California Enterprises, Inc.*, 98 Nita App. 2d 240, 250 (2d Dist. 1950); *McChristian v. Popkin*, 75 Nita App. 2d 249, 256–257 (2d Dist. 1946).

Here, the complainant alleges that Schmit is a managing agent and furthermore, that Walsh, as president of Pacific Quad, Inc., ratified Schmit's conduct. If the appellant can prove either of these allegations and further prove oppression, fraud, or malice, she would be entitled to punitive damages.

Judgment reversed and case remanded to the trial court for further proceedings consistent with this opinion.

PROPOSED JURY INSTRUCTIONS

This case file may be used for a full trial on the issue of liability only, or on both the issues of liability and damages. If used solely for the issue of liability, the proposed jury instructions should be modified accordingly by deleting instructions 2.17–2.23, plus either 2.15 (to use federal law) or 2.16 (to use California law). Although the employer is too small to come under the federal anti-discrimination statute (Title VII), the case can be tried under a state law that adopts either the federal or California approach on what effect to give an employer's anti-harassment policies, by selecting the appropriate jury instruction. When using the file to try both liability and damages, to apply federal law, omit instructions 2.15 and 2.21; to apply California law, omit instruction 2.16.

PART I. PRELIMINARY INSTRUCTIONS

1.01–MEMBERS OF THE JURY

You have been selected as jurors and have taken an oath to well and truly try this case. This trial will last one day.

During the trial there will be times when the court takes breaks, called recesses. During these times you must not talk about this case among yourselves or with anyone else.

During the trial, do not talk to any of the plaintiffs or defendants, their lawyers, or any of the witnesses.

If anyone tries to talk to you about any of the matters under consideration in this trial, you should immediately report it to the court.

You should keep an open mind. You should not form or express a final opinion on any issue during the trial. You should keep from reaching a conclusion on the case until you have heard all the evidence, the arguments of the attorneys, and the final instructions on the law that I will give you at the end of the case.

1.02–CONDUCT OF THE TRIAL

First, the attorneys will have an opportunity to make opening statements. These statements should be considered only as a preview of what the attorneys expect the evidence in the trial will be. Opening statements are not evidence.

Next, witnesses will be called to testify. They will be placed under oath and questioned by the attorneys.

During the trial, I might receive documents and other exhibits as evidence. If evidence is given to you to examine, you should examine it carefully, one person at a time, and without any comment.

It is the attorneys' right and duty to object when testimony or other evidence is being offered that they believe should not be admitted. When I decide that an objection is correct, I will sustain it, and you should proceed as if you never saw the evidence, or heard the attorney's question, or the witness's answer, if given. There also may be times when I will strike evidence from the record; you should act as if this evidence never existed.

If I decide that an objection is not correct, I will overrule it. You should give that evidence no more weight than if the objection had not been made.

After all the witnesses have testified, the attorneys will make final arguments. These statements are not evidence. The attorneys are, however, permitted to try to persuade you to decide on a verdict in their client's favor. You may accept or reject these arguments as you see fit.

Finally, just before you retire to consider your verdict, I will give you further instructions on the law that applies to this case.

PART II. FINAL INSTRUCTIONS

2.01

It is now my duty to instruct you in the law that applies to this case. It is your duty to follow the law. You must apply the law according to the way I state it in these instructions. You must consider all the instructions as a whole; you may not single out certain instructions and disregard others. (CALIFORNIA JURY INSTRUCTIONS, CIVIL: BOOK OF APPROVED JURY INSTRUCTIONS (BAJI) 1.00, 1.01 (West Pub. Co. 2003); NITA 1:01)

As jurors it is your duty to determine the facts and to determine them only from the evidence in this case. Once you determine what the facts of the case are, you must apply the law to them. You must not let any sympathy or prejudice affect your decisions. You must arrive at your verdict by a unanimous vote or a vote of (insert number if applicable). (BAJI 1.00)

2.02

From time to time the court has ruled on the admissibility of evidence. You must not concern yourselves with the reasons for these rulings. You must act as though you never knew of questions or exhibits that one of the attorneys withdrew or that I refused or struck. (NITA 1:01, BAJI 1.02)

2.03

At some points in the trial I called your attention to matters that were admitted for only limited purposes. You must not consider these matters for anything else. (BAJI 2.05)

2.04

The attorneys have made opening and closing statements to you. They were only used to acquaint you with the case and allow the lawyers to present their ideas about how you should judge the evidence. None of these statements are evidence. You are to use them only for guidance in determining the facts. (NITA 1:02)

2.05

The testimony of witnesses is evidence. You as jurors are the sole judges of the believability of the witnesses. You may consider any matter that makes you think the witness is being more or less truthful. Some examples are:

- The way the witness looks and sounds;

- The witness's ability and opportunity to perceive the event that he or she testified to;

- The character of the witness for honesty or dishonesty;

- The existence of bias, self-interest, or prejudice;

- Whether the testimony sounds reasonable in light of all the other evidence;

- A statement made by the witness, either before this trial or in court today, that is not consistent with any part of the witness's testimony.
(BAJI 2.20, NITA 1:03)

2.06

You have heard evidence by a witness who testified as an expert. The law allows experts to express opinions on subjects involving their special knowledge, training, and experience. When evaluating her opinions, you should consider her qualifications, the bases and reasons for her opinions, and generally how believable she was. (BAJI 2.40, NITA 1:04)

2.07

There are two kinds of evidence: direct and circumstantial. Both are equally valid.

Direct evidence is evidence that by itself would establish a fact in question. A common example is the testimony of an eyewitness.

Circumstantial evidence is evidence that does not prove the fact in question directly, but which requires that you apply your own common knowledge and experience to it in order to establish the fact in question. A common example is a human footprint, which by itself does not prove that a certain person was present, but it allows you to infer that fact.

The law makes no distinction between direct and circumstantial evidence as to the degree or amount of proof required. Both kinds of evidence should be considered according to whatever weight or value you decide it has. (NITA 1:05, BAJI 2.00)

2.08

I have made a number of remarks and rulings during the trial. You are not to take my comments as an indication that I have any opinion about the facts or about what your verdict should be. (NITA 1:06)

2.09

You must apply the law as I am instructing you. Regardless of any opinions you may have as to what the law ought to be, it would be a violation of your sworn duty to consider any other view of the law other than that which I am giving you in these instructions. (NITA 1:06)

2.10

When determining the facts, however, you should consider the evidence in the light of your own observations and experiences in life. (NITA 1:01)

2.11

One of the parties in this case is a corporation, and you must give it the same fair treatment as an individual under similar circumstances. (NITA 2:02)

2.12

Now I am about to move on to the laws applying specifically to this case. When I use the expression "if you find" I mean that you must be persuaded that the issue in question is more probably true than not true. (NITA 2:01)

2.13

The plaintiff, Alice Rowe, claims she was injured by the alleged sexual harassment of Stanley Schmit, in violation of the Nita Government Code. The Code states that it is unlawful for an employer to harass an employee in a sexual way. The Code says that sexual harassment includes verbal, physical, and visual harassment, and unwanted sexual advances.

2.14

For Alice Rowe to prove her claim, you must be convinced that it is more likely than not that the following facts actually happened:

First, that Stanley Schmit engaged in unwanted sexual conduct. To find this there is a three-part test:

(a) that the acts, gestures, or language complained of actually occurred;

(b) that Stanley Schmit's conduct was "unwanted" by the plaintiff. You are to judge this from the viewpoint of the plaintiff;

(c) that Stanley Schmit's conduct was in fact sexual. You are to judge this from the viewpoint of a reasonable person in those circumstances. That is, you must ask yourselves: Would a reasonable person in these circumstances interpret Stanley Schmit's conduct as sexual?

Second, if you have decided that Stanley Schmit engaged in unwanted sexual conduct, you must determine whether the plaintiff was deprived of an employment benefit by the acts of sexual harassment. You must be convinced that it is more likely than not that the plaintiff either lost her job as a result of the sexual harassment or that the harassment created a hostile work environment for the plaintiff.

There are two ways that you may find the plaintiff lost her job as a result of the sexual harassment:

(a) You may find that she was fired for her refusal to give in to Stanley Schmit's sexual demands. This is called termination.

(b) Or you may find that she quit, and was reasonable in quitting, because the sexual harassment made it intolerable for her to continue working there. This is called constructive termination.

Even if the plaintiff's loss of her job was not due to the sexual harassment, according to the two tests I just described, you may also find that the plaintiff was deprived of an employment benefit if she was subjected to a hostile work environment. You must judge this from the viewpoint of the plaintiff and determine whether she felt the sexual harassment created an intimidating, oppressive, or offensive atmosphere that interfered with her well-being or her ability to perform her work, and if she did, whether she was reasonable in reacting in this way.

Third, you must find either that Stanley Schmit was a supervisor at Pacific Quad, Inc., or that the company knew or should have known of the sexual harassment, but failed to take any corrective action.

2.15 [CALIFORNIA INSTRUCTION]

If you find it is more likely than not that the three elements of sexual harassment on which I just instructed you are true, then your verdict should be for the plaintiff. If you find it is more likely than not that any one of these three elements is not true, then your verdict should be for the defendant, and your consideration of this case will be complete.

2.16 [FEDERAL INSTRUCTION]

If you find it is more likely than not that the three elements of sexual harassment on which I just instructed you are true, you must enter a verdict for the plaintiff unless you find that the defendant has proven an affirmative defense.

The affirmative defense offered by the defendant in this case is (1) that the defendant had an effective anti-harassment policy and (2) that the plaintiff unreasonably failed to use it. The defendant must prove each of these two elements by a preponderance of the evidence. If you find that the defendant has proven an affirmative defense, then your verdict should be for the defendant, and your consideration of this case will be complete.

If you find that it is more likely than not that the three elements of sexual harassment on which I just instructed you are true and that the defendant has not proven an affirmative defense, then your verdict should be for the plaintiff.

2.17

If your verdict is for the plaintiff, you must decide how much money she should be awarded. The plaintiff alleges that she suffered economic loss from an unlawful termination of her job, plus humiliation, embarrassment, and emotional distress.

2.18

If you find that the plaintiff was unlawfully terminated—in other words, that she either was fired or was forced to quit—you should award her a sum that will reasonably make up for her lost wages and employment benefits during the period between the time she stopped working and the time of your verdict.

This, however, depends on whether the plaintiff attempted to find another suitable job after leaving the defendant's company. This is called "mitigation." If you find that the plaintiff was unable to seek work or unable to work because of emotional distress caused by the sexual harassment, she is excused from her duty to mitigate her losses, and you should award her full back pay for this period when she was unable to work. If the plaintiff has earned wages since leaving defendant's company, you should subtract this amount from her total award of back pay.

2.19

If you find that the plaintiff paid money for personal or career counseling as a result of the sexual harassment, you should award her a sum that will reasonably reimburse her for these expenses. If you find that she would have incurred some of these expenses despite the sexual harassment, you should award her a sum that will reasonably reimburse her for only those expenses that are directly a result of the sexual harassment.

2.20

If you find that the plaintiff suffered any emotional distress as a result of the sexual harassment, you should award her a sum that will reasonably compensate her for it. Emotional distress includes factors such as humiliation, embarrassment, stress, insomnia, depression, and nightmares.

2.21 [CALIFORNIA]

If you find that the plaintiff suffered damages, you must consider whether the consequences of those damages were avoidable to the plaintiff through any anti-harassment policy the defendant had. To find that the plaintiff's damages were avoidable, the defendant must establish three elements: (1) the employer took reasonable steps to prevent and correct workplace sexual harassment; (2) the employee unreasonably failed to use the preventive and corrective measures that the employer provided; and (3) reasonable use of the employer's procedures would have prevented at least some of the harm that the employee suffered. This defense will allow the defendant to escape liability for those damages, and only those damages, that the plaintiff more likely than not could have prevented with reasonable effort and without undue risk, expense, or humiliation, by taking advantage of the employer's internal complaint procedures appropriately designed to prevent and eliminate sexual harassment.

2.22

The plaintiff is also seeking what are called punitive damages. The law permits you, the jury, to award an injured person punitive damages in order to punish a wrongdoer for some extraordinary misconduct and to serve as an example or warning to others not to engage in such conduct. There are two parts to the test for punitive damages:

(a) You must find that the sexual harassment was carried out with intent, oppression, fraud, or malice; and

(b) You must determine either that Stanley Schmit was a managing agent of Pacific Quad or that John Walsh ratified the actions of Stanley Schmit.

   (i) You should find that Stanley Schmit was a managing agent if he had the kind of authority at Pacific Quad that authorized him to take part in running the company. Examples of a managing agent's role are: hiring and firing employees, disciplining employees, and purchasing major items for the company.

   (ii) You should find that John Walsh ratified the actions of Stanley Schmit if John Walsh approved of those actions, or if he was informed of Stanley Schmit's actions but failed to try to make up for the harm done.

You may award punitive damages in any sum that you agree is proper. However, punitive damages should bear a reasonable relation to the amount awarded for economic loss and emotional distress. (BAJI 7.12)

2.23

If your verdict is for the plaintiff, but you determine that she has suffered no economic loss or emotional distress and that she should not receive punitive damages, you shall award her nominal damages in the sum of one dollar.

2.24

You are now to begin your deliberations. I recommend that you begin by choosing a foreperson— that is, one of you should be selected to guide the discussion and try to make your decision making as smooth as possible. The foreperson should not, however, have any greater say in the final decisions than any other juror. (BAJI 15.52)

2.25

As soon as all of you or (insert number if applicable) of you have agreed on the verdict and, if necessary, the amount of money to be awarded, you should return to the court room, and the foreperson will be asked to read your decision. (BAJI 15.52)

IN THE SUPERIOR COURT OF DARROW COUNTY, NITA

CIVIL DIVISION

ALICE ROWE,   )
Plaintiff.   )
)   Civ. No. O-9876543
)
v.   )   JURY VERDICT
)
Pacific Quad, Inc.,   )
Defendant.   )

We, the Jury, return the following verdict, and each of us concurs in this verdict: (Choose the appropriate verdict)

I.

We, the Jury, find for the plaintiff, Alice Rowe, and against the defendant, Pacific Quad, Inc., in the sum of $ _____, of which $ _____ shall be awarded as punitive damages.

_____

Foreperson

II.

We, the Jury, find for the defendant, Pacific Quad, Inc., and against the plaintiff, Alice Rowe.

_____

Foreperson

NATIONAL INSTITUTE FOR TRIAL ADVOCACY